General editor: Graham Handley MA Ph.D.

Brodie's Notes on William Shakespeare's

Julius Caesar

T. W. Smith BA
Former English Master, Barrow and Teignmouth Grammar Schools

MACMILLAN

First published 1985 by Pan Books Ltd
This revised edition first published 1990
by Pan Books Ltd

Published 1993 by
THE MACMILLAN PRESS LTD
Houndmills, Basingstoke, Hampshire RG21 2XS
and London
Companies and representatives
throughout the world

ISBN 0-333-58174-1

Printed in Great Britain by
Cox and Wyman Ltd
Reading, Berks

Contents

Line references in these Notes are to the
Arden Shakespeare: Julius Caesar,
but as references are given to particular
acts and scenes, the Notes may be used with any
edition of the play.

Preface

This student revision aid is based on the principle that in any close examination of Shakespeare's plays 'the text's the thing'. Seeing a performance, or listening to a tape or record of a performance, is essential and is in itself a valuable and stimulating experience in understanding and appreciation. However, a real evaluation of Shakespeare's greatness, of his universality and of the nature of his literary and dramatic art, can only be achieved by constant application to the texts of the plays themselves. These revised editions of Brodie's Notes are intended to supplement that process through detailed critical commentary.

The first aim of each book is to fix the whole play in the reader's mind by providing a concise summary of the plot, relating it back, where appropriate, to its source or sources. Subsequently the book provides a summary of each scene, followed by *critical comments*. These may convey its importance in the dramatic structure of the play, creation of atmosphere, indication of character development, significance of figurative language etc, and they will also explain or paraphrase difficult words or phrases and identify meaningful references. At the end of each act revision questions are set to test the student's specific and broad understanding and appreciation of the play.

An extended critical commentary follows this scene by scene analysis. This embraces such major elements as characterization, imagery, the use of blank verse and prose, soliloquies and other aspects of the play which the editor considers need close attention. The paramount aim is to send the reader back to the text. The book concludes with a series of revision questions which require a detailed knowledge of the play; the first of these has notes by the editor of what *might* be included in a written answer. The intention is to stimulate and to guide; the whole emphasis of this commentary is to encourage the student's *involvement* in the play, to develop disciplined critical responses and thus promote personal enrichment through the imaginative experience of our greatest writer.

Graham Handley

Shakespeare and the Elizabethan playhouse

William Shakespeare was born in Stratford-upon-Avon in 1564, and there are reasons to suppose that he came from a relatively prosperous family. He was probably educated at Stratford Grammar School and, at the age of eighteen, married Anne Hathaway, who was twenty-six. They had three children, a girl born shortly after their marriage, followed by twins in 1585 (the boy died in 1596). It seems likely that Shakespeare left for London shortly after a company of visiting players had visited Stratford in 1585, for by 1592 – according to the jealous testimony of one of his fellow-writers Robert Greene – he was certainly making his way both as actor and dramatist. The theatres were closed because of the plague in 1593; when they reopened Shakespeare worked with the Lord Chamberlain's men, later the King's Men, and became a shareholder in each of the two theatres with which he was most closely associated, the Globe and the Blackfriars. He later purchased New Place, a considerable property in his home town of Stratford, to which he retired in 1611; there he entertained his great contemporary Ben Jonson (1572–1637) and the poet Michael Drayton (1563–1631). An astute businessman, Shakespeare lived comfortably in the town until his death in 1616.

This is a very brief outline of the life of our greatest writer, for little more can be said of him with certainty, though the plays – and poems – are living witness to the wisdom, humanity and many-faceted nature of the man. He was both popular and successful as a dramatist, perhaps less so as an actor. He probably began work as a dramatist in the late 1580s, by collaborating with other playwrights and adapting old plays, and by 1598 Francis Meres was paying tribute to his excellence in both comedy and tragedy. His first original play was probably *Love's Labour's Lost* (1590) and while the theatres were closed during the plague he wrote his narrative poems *Venus and Adonis* (1593) and *The Rape of Lucrece* (1594). The sonnets were almost certainly written in the 1590s though not published until 1609; the first 126 seem to be addressed to a young man who was his friend and patron, while the rest are concerned with the 'dark lady'.

The dating of Shakespeare's plays has exercised scholars ever since the publication of the First Folio (1623), which listed them as comedies, histories and tragedies. It seems more important to look at them chronologically as far as possible, in order to trace Shakespeare's considerable development as a dramatist. The first period, say to the middle of the 1590s, included such plays as *Love's Labour's Lost*, *The Comedy of Errors*, *Richard III*, *The Taming of the Shrew*, *Romeo and Juliet* and *Richard II*. These early plays embrace the categories listed in the First Folio, so that Shakespeare the craftsman is evident in his capacity for variety of subject and treatment. The next phase includes *A Midsummer Night's Dream*, *The Merchant of Venice*, *Henry IV Parts 1 and 2*, *Henry V* and *Much Ado About Nothing*, as well as *Julius Caesar*, *As You Like It* and *Twelfth Night*. These are followed, in the early years of the 17th century, by his great tragic period: *Hamlet*, *Othello*, *King Lear* and *Macbeth*, with *Antony and Cleopatra* and *Coriolanus* belonging to 1607–09. The final phase embraces the romances (1610–13), *Cymbeline*, *The Tempest* and *The Winter's Tale* and the historical play *Henry VIII*.

Each of these revision aids will place the individual text under examination in the chronology of the remarkable dramatic output that spanned twenty years from the early 1590s to about 1613. The practical theatre for which Shakespeare wrote and acted derived from the inn courtyards in which performances had taken place, the few playhouses in his day being modelled on their structure. They were circular or hexagonal in shape, allowing the balconies and boxes around the walls full view of the stage. This large stage, which had no scenery, jutted out into the pit, the most extensive part of the theatre, where the poorer people – the 'groundlings' – stood. There was no roof (though the Blackfriars, used from 1608 onwards, was an indoor theatre) and thus bad weather meant no performance. Certain plays were acted at court, and these private performances normally marked some special occasion. Costumes, often rich ones, were used, and music was a common feature, with musicians on or under the stage; this sometimes had additional features, for example a trapdoor to facilitate the entry of a ghost. Women were barred by law from appearing on stage, and all female parts were played by boy actors; this undoubtedly explains the many instances in Shakespeare where a woman has to conceal her identity by disguising

herself as a man, e.g. Rosalind in *As You Like It*, Viola in *Twelfth Night*.

Shakespeare and his contemporaries often adapted their plays from sources in history and literature, extending an incident or a myth or creating a dramatic narrative from known facts. They were always aware of their own audiences, and frequently included topical references, sometimes of a satirical flavour, which would appeal to – and be understood by – the groundlings as well as their wealthier patrons who occupied the boxes. Shakespeare obviously learned much from his fellow dramatists and actors, being on good terms with many of them. Ben Jonson paid generous tribute to him in the lines prefaced to the First Folio of Shakespeare's plays:

Thou art a monument without a tomb,
And art alive still, while thy book doth live
And we have wits to read, and praise to give.

Among his contemporaries were Thomas Kyd (1558–94) and Christopher Marlowe (1564–93). Kyd wrote *The Spanish Tragedy*, the revenge motif here foreshadowing the much more sophisticated treatment evident in *Hamlet*, while Marlowe evolved the 'mighty line' of blank verse, a combination of natural speech and elevated poetry. The quality and variety of Shakespeare's blank verse owes something to the innovatory brilliance of Marlowe but carries the stamp of individuality, richness of association, technical virtuosity and, above all, the genius of imaginative power.

The texts of Shakespeare's plays are still rich sources for scholars, and the editors of these revision aids have used the Arden editions of Shakespeare, which are regarded as pre-eminent for their scholarly approach. They are strongly recommended for advanced students, but other editions, like The New Penguin Shakespeare, The New Swan, The Signet are all good annotated editions currently available. A reading list of selected reliable works on the play being studied is provided at the end of each commentary and students are advised to turn to these as their interest in the play deepens.

Literary terms used in these notes

Simile The discovery of a striking resemblance between two objects, attitudes or actions that otherwise differ from each other, introduced by 'like' or 'as'. The second object, which should be familiar, throws new and often picturesque light on the first. It is not an ordinary comparison, but a deliberate poetic device: 'like a deer strucken by many princes'; 'as a dish fit for the gods'.

Metaphor Essentially this is a condensed simile: the second object is substituted for the first. In III, 1, 260 '(thy wounds) like dumb mouths' is a simile; in III, 2, 227 'poor dumb mouths' is a metaphor. True metaphors (i.e. not absorbed into everyday language) are rare in this play: 'beads of sorrow' (i.e. tears), III, 1, 284.

Personification Treating inanimate objects or abstract ideas as persons (usually indicated by a capital initial letter): 'chastisement doth therefore hide his head' (IV, 3, 16).

Apostrophe Addressing a person or personified idea as if he or it were present: 'O grief,/Where hast thou led me?' (I, 3, 111).

Analogy The use of a similar action or situation as an illustration (looser than a simile). Caesar is presented in various guises in the form of analogies: Cassius sees him at one moment as the Colossus of Rhodes and the next as a feeble old man being carried to safety; Caesar sees himself as an immovable North Star; Antony sees him, as he lies dead at the feet of his assassins, as a noble stag with whose lifeblood the hunters have daubed themselves.

Anachronism Reference to an object or person not in existence at the time: 'The clock hath stricken three' (II, 1, 192; see also II, 2, 114).

Antithesis The balancing of opposite ideas in parallel phrases or clauses to emphasize their difference:
'*Cowards* die *many times* before their deaths;/The *valiant* never taste of death but *once*.' (II, 2, 32)

Chiasmus The second part reverses the order of the first:
'Pardon, Caesar; Caesar, pardon' (III, 1, 55).

Climax The arrangement of three or more objects in ascending order of importance (the Greek word means 'ladder'). See *Structure* and Brutus's speech to the crowd (III, 2, 25). In an *anti-climax* the last element is contradictory or absurd.

Cognate Used of words from the same root, e.g. 'hale' and 'heal'.

Consonance Intentional repetition of the same consonant in two or more words close together: Domestic fury and fierce civil strife. The repetition of initial sounds is *alliteration*, frequent in English verse, but scarce in *Julius Caesar*. In *onomatopoeia* sounds are imitated: 'battle hurtled' (II, 2, 22)

Historic Present A past event is narrated in the present tense for greater vividness.

Hypallage An epithet is transferred from a living person to an associated object; human feeling is credited to something inanimate: 'captive bonds' (I, 1, 34).

Hyperbole Exaggeration for the sake of emphasis: 'Hence! wilt thou lift up Olympus?' (III, 1, 74).

Irony Expressing the opposite of what is really meant, e.g. pretended praise spoken in mockery: 'The choice and master spirits of this age' (III, 1, 163).

Dramatic irony See *Structure*.

Elegy Poem of mourning and praise for the dead: Antony over Brutus.

Rhetorical question Question to which the answer, being so obvious, is not expected: 'Who is here so base, that would be a bondman?' (III, 2, 30).

Tautology Repetition of the same meaning in different words, either deliberately or unconsciously: 'The fortunes and affairs of noble Brutus' (III, 1, 135).

Soliloquy Thinking aloud on the stage, alone or unheard by others: a dramatist's method of revealing real feelings or attitudes. Brutus manages five in Act II Scene 1; Cassius and Antony expose another side of their characters in I, 2, 305 and III, 1, 253.

The play
Plot, source and treatment

Plot

The popular dictator Julius Caesar is celebrating a triumph but republican partisans are secretly opposed to his growing power, and there intrudes upon the scene of pomp and splendour the mysterious warning, 'Beware the ides of March'.

The fears of Brutus, a noble Roman, are played upon by Cassius, who envies Caesar his greatness, and his arguments are reinforced by Casca's account of the offer of a crown to the dictator, who, however, has refused it out of regard for popular feeling, which abhors the name of king.

That night, a stormy one full of portents, Cassius gathers his band of conspirators. They meet at the house of Brutus, whom they mean to choose as leader because of his reputation for honesty. Accepting leadership, Brutus forces his decisions upon the others, deciding that only Caesar shall be killed.

Next morning, the ides of March, Caesar is reluctant to attend the meeting of the Senate (owing to his wife's dream), but is persuaded to appear by Decius, one of the conspirators. When Caesar has taken his seat, the whole band press round him in support of a petition they know he will refuse. At a given signal they all stab him and proclaim liberty to the Senate, which flees in a body.

Caesar's lieutenant Antony, who has been detained from the meeting, appears under a safe-conduct and secures from Brutus permission to deliver a public oration at Caesar's funeral, promising to throw no blame on the conspirators. Speaking after Brutus, Antony keeps to the letter of his promise, until the crowd understand his ironical references to the 'honourable men' and, enraged by the spectacle of Caesar's scarred corpse and stirred by the generous terms of his will, they riot. Brutus and Cassius flee from Rome.

Antony, Lepidus (another general) and young Octavius, Caesar's heir, draw up a black-list of their enemies; meanwhile Brutus and Cassius have raised armies in the East. A bitter quarrel between these two is followed by a reconciliation but fate seems against them. Brutus, oppressed by a visit from Caesar's ghost, is impatient to settle the issue with Antony and Octavius on the plains of Philippi. His wing is victorious over Octavius, but Cassius, defeated by Antony, kills himself under a misapprehension. The conflict is renewed, and this time Brutus is driven from the field to commit suicide in his turn. The spirit of Caesar is avenged.

Source

Julius Caesar, like its sequel *Antony and Cleopatra* and that other Roman tragedy *Coriolanus*, in which the citizens figure more prominently, was taken from a version of Plutarch's *Lives* by Sir Thomas North, a slightly older contemporary of Shakespeare's. This was a translation of a French translation from the Greek by Jacques Amyot (1513-93); first published in 1579, it was widely read.

Plutarch, a Greek student of Roman history, who died c. AD140, produced a number of parallel lives, Greek and Roman heroes being paired off: Caesar is matched with Alexander the Great, Brutus with a philosopher who expelled a tyrant and Antony with a dissipated adventurer of military genius. Plutarch was less interested in historical accuracy than in the bearing of character upon destiny, which has given an appeal for all time to his stories. He was rather prejudiced in favour of his countrymen and inclined to emphasize the foibles of the Romans. By his day, however, Caesar and his exploits had become legendary, and Plutarch had no hesitation in twinning him with Alexander. The fifth month of the Roman year had been renamed Julius, as if he were a god.

Cassius's spiteful accounts of Caesar's physical weaknesses are distorted by Shakespeare out of instances in Plutarch which give a very different picture: Caesar actually kept his body fit by severe training; he had no attack of epilepsy in front of a crowd; nor was he deaf. In Act II Scene 2 he is made to appear indecisive and swayed by omens, but superstition was rife in ancient Rome and omens were common topics of conversation. Actually in this scene he is deterred only once from going to the meeting, and that is in response to his wife on her knees, like Brutus's wife in the previous scene. What makes him reaffirm his original decision is less Decius's interpretation of Calphurnia's dream (or even the Senate's prospective offer of the coveted title), than the thought of his being called a coward and by the Senate of all people! He was prepared to dismiss contemptuously the meeting he had summoned them to, and certainly the Senate deserved such scorn when (in Plutarch) it ignored his cry for help and made itself scarce. We find, too, in Plutarch the hint that Caesar was depressed and almost fatalistic about his future – he deliberately refused the services of a bodyguard, which could easily have been supplied from his soldiery:

> death, a necessary end,
> Will come when it will come.

Plutarch's concluding comparison of Alexander and Caesar indicates that both brilliant generals inspired great confidence in their troops, however arduous the campaigns that brought victories and booty, and both were cut off at the height of their careers. There is one subtle difference: Alexander was admired even by his enemies; Caesar inspired hatred on the part of many of his fellow-citizens (note the size of the proscription, IV, 3, 174) and of some of his personal friends.

His most dangerous 'ambition' (dangerous for him) was to receive the hated title of 'king', and he must have been thinking of a dynasty when he wanted the barren Calphurnia to give him an heir. Ironically the *name* of Caesar itself was to achieve royal status in the titles of two crowned sovereigns whose dynasties have since foundered – the Kaiser and the Tsar.

Treatment

A famous and rather complicated period of Roman history has been skilfully condensed by the world's greatest dramatist into a plot that is one of the best constructed among his plays. The issue is clear cut, and the action moves steadily, and in some places swiftly, to its predestined end. Historical intervals are drastically shortened without, however, leaving any noticeable gaps in the framework. Living characters are created by the transformation of lively though often discursive narrative into stage dialogue, as well as the ingenious use of random hints and references.

Whereas Shakespeare has followed the *Lives* more closely than he followed Holinshed (upon whom he drew for his English historical plays) – much of this play has, indeed, been described as 'Plutarch dramatized' – yet he made certain alterations chiefly in the interest of *unity of action*, e.g.:

1 The triumph in October, 45 BC, and the feast of the Lupercalia in February, 44 BC, are combined in one day, apparently March 14th.

2 On the *next* day, March 15th, i.e. the Ides of March, the assassination, the funeral (actually two days later) and the arrival of Octavius (in May) all take place.

3 The will, in Plutarch made public *before* the funeral, is read by Antony over Caesar's body.

4 The greatest simplification of all is that the Triumvirate, who did not meet till October of the following year at Bologna, after months of civil war among themselves, begin their proscription and campaign as if fresh from executing Caesar's will.

5 The quarrels between Brutus and Cassius are composed in one grand reconciliation.

6 The two battles at Philippi, separated by twenty days (the Spirit appearing again on the eve of the second), are condensed into two actions on the same day.

The student who consults Plutarch will notice how often, where Shakespeare might safely have invented for himself, he has 'lifted' whole incidents, as well as ideas and expressions, straight into his play. This is particularly noticeable in Act V, where there is little scope for the 'alchemy' of poetry in the bustle of action. The following extracts may illustrate the materials for which Shakespeare was indebted to Plutarch, without detracting from the genius that transmuted them into immortal verse:

They durst not come to him themselves to tell him what they would have him to do, but in the night did cast sundrie papers into the Praetors seate where he gave audience, and the most of them to this effect: Thou sleepest Brutus, and art not Brutus indeed. Cassius finding Brutus ambition stirred up the more by these seditious bils, did pricke him forward, and egge him on the more, for a private quarrel he had conceived against Caesar ... Caesar also had Cassius in great ielousie, and suspected him much ... as for those fat men and smooth combed heads, quoth he, I never reckon of them: but these pale visaged and carion leane people, I feare them most. (Act I Scene 2).

Then perceiving that her husband was marvellously out of quiet, and that he could take no rest ... she spake in this sort unto him: I being, O Brutus, (said she) the daughter of Cato, was maried unto thee, not to be thy bed-fellowe ... but to be partaker also with thee of thy good and evill fortune . . . I confesse, that a womans wit commonly is too weake to keepe a secret safely: but . . . for myself, I have this benefite moreover, that I am the daughter of Cato and the wife of Brutus . . .With those wordes she shewed him her wound on her thigh, and told him what she had done to prove herself. (Act II Scene 1).

(Decius) reproved Caesar, saying: that he gave the Senate occasion to mislike with him, and that they might think he mocked them, considering that by his commandement they were all assembled, and that they were ready willingly to . . . proclaime him king of all the provinces of the Empire of Rome out of Italy. And furthermore, that if any man should tell them from him, they should depart for that present time, and returne again when Calpurnia should have better dreames: what would his enemies and ill-willers say? . . . Therewithal he tooke Caesar by the hand, and brought him out of his house. (Act II Scene 2).

Afterwards, when Caesar's body was brought into the market place, Antonius making his funeral oration in praise of the dead according to the auncient custome of Rome, and perceiving that his words moved the common people to compassion: he framed his eloquence to make their hearts yerne the more, and taking Caesar's gowne all bloudy in his hand, he layed it open to the sight of them all, shewing what a number of cuts and holes it had upon it. Therewithal the people fell presently into such a rage and mutinie, that there was no more order kept amongst the common people. (Act III Scene 2).

Brutus was a careful man and slept very little . . . one night very late . . . as he was in his tent with a little light, thinking of waightie matters: he thought he heard one come in to him, and casting his eye towards the doore of his tent, that he saw a wonderfull straunge and monstrous shape of a bodie comming towards him, and sayed never a word. So Brutus boldly asked him what he was, a god or a man, and what cause brought him thither. The spirit aunswered him. I am thy evill Spirit, Brutus: and thou shalt see me by the citie of Philippes. Brutus being no otherwise afraid, replied againe unto it: Well, then I shall see thee againe. The spirit presently vanished away: and Brutus called his men unto him, who told him that they heard no noise, nor saw any thing at all. (Act IV Scene 3).

Where Shakespeare has deviated in matters of detail from the original work, the intention has obviously been to stress some feature in one of his characters or bring out a contrast, e.g.:

1 Brutus is given the credit of requiring no oath.
2 Marcellus and Flavius are executed instead of merely losing their appointments as tribunes – the act of a 'tyrant'.
3 Cicero (at the height of his fame) is used in a minor role, mainly as a foil to Casca, while the Senate appear once only in a very supernumerary capacity.

4 Caesar acquires a touch of nobility by rejecting Artemidorus's petition, instead of being prevented from reading it.

5 Instead of the conspirators being given a safe-conduct from the Capitol, it is Antony who ventures forth and shows his resourcefulness.

6 In Plutarch Caesar's funeral was according to custom, not an act of grace on the part of Brutus, whose speech was actually made immediately after the assassination and received in silence.

7 The poet's instrusion does not break off the quarrel between Brutus and Cassius, as in Plutarch, but comes as a comic interlude after their *better natures* have surmounted their differences.

8 The vein of cruelty in Cassius is emphasized by his *killing* his standard-bearer.

9 Pindarus, not his short-sighted master, misunderstands the alighting of Titinius, but his description of what he sees serves in the play to inform the audience.

10 The Portia of history took her own life *after* her husband's death.

Title, text and date of *Julius Caesar*

Title

Brutus has all the characteristics of a tragic hero. A noble character stoops to conspiracy and, by errors of judgement, the product of his unpractical idealism, brings on himself and others defeat and death. Why not, then, *The Tragedy of Brutus*? Caesar dies halfway through the play and Brutus receives the final tribute.

The answer to that question must be put briefly. This, the first of the Roman plays, follows closely on the English Histories, in which the monarch gives his name to the drama enacted in his reign, however great or small the part he plays in it. What more natural than that the Roman dictator should follow suit? The suggestion may be added that, just as the Roman citizens were more affected than anything else by Caesar's 'poor dumb mouths', so the main thing for which an Elizabethan audience would assemble would be to see 'Caesar bleed in sport'.

Moreover, the choice is justified structurally. The balance of the plot gives no one of the chief characters, not even Brutus, absolute predominance over the others. The central theme, and the climax, is the assassination of Julius Caesar. The first two acts are concerned with the preparation, the last two with the retribution. It is interesting to note here that Plutarch's *Life of Julius Caesar* ends with the suicide of Brutus.

Further, Caesar's influence is felt even more powerfully after his death than in his life: as Brutus says (V,3,94), 'O Julius Caesar, thou art mighty yet!' And at the end the imperial crown is secured for Octavius.

Text

Few readers of Shakespeare realize the difficulties scholars have had to overcome in order to establish accurate texts of the plays. The First Folio of 1623 contained thirty-six plays. Other collected editions or Folios were published in the seventeenth century, the Third and Fourth Folios containing seven additional plays, none of which, with the exception of *Pericles*, is now thought to be by Shakespeare. Sixteen of the plays had already been published separately as Quartos before 1623, and in the case of some plays, for example *Hamlet*, more than one Quarto edition exists. Some of these Quartos are almost word for word the same as the texts in the First Folio and were possibly set up from Shakespeare's own manuscript or at least from accurate theatre copies; but others are shortened, inferior versions, possibly 'pirated' editions published by some unathorized person who had access to theatre copies or parts of them, or who had taken down the plays in shorthand while they were being performed.

It is thought that the texts of the First Folio were set up from the good Quartos and from good theatre copies. But these texts must all be compared, printers' mistakes and other interference traced, before a reliable text can be arrived at. Such a task has been unnecessary in the case of *Julius Caesar*, as the first known edition is that of the First Folio, and the text has very few doubtful passages. All the acts of *Julius Caesar* are marked in the First Folio, but no scenes, except Sc. 1 at the start, which obviously serves no purpose by itself.

The first editor to attempt the problem of the text was Nicholas Rowe (1674-1718), who also divided most of the plays into acts and scenes, supplied place names of the location of each scene, indications of entrances and exits and a list of dramatis personae, which are absent from many of the texts in the Quarto and folio editions.

Date

Two contemporary references to *Julius Caesar* place its first stage production in the autumn of 1599 in the newly built Globe Theatre. This would be soon after *Henry V*, the last of Shakespeare's plays featuring the English kings; this hero-monarch was only two years older than Alexander when he died at the height of his career.

Scene summaries, critical commentary, textual notes and revision questions

Act I Scene 1

A crowd of workmen, having downed tools for Caesar's celebration of his latest victory, are encountered by two tribunes Flavius and Marullus. When rebuked for making the day a holiday, they leave it to their spokesman the Cobbler who first dodges the issue with a string of puns, and then admits that they are on the streets to see Caesar pass. Marullus upbraids them for so easily forgetting the great reception they gave Pompey, and for rejoicing at Caesar's victory over their former hero; he bids them pray to the gods for forgiveness. Flavius goes further, and calls upon them to assemble by the Tiber and shed tears into it. After the crowd's subdued departure, Flavius tells Marullus to join him in removing Caesar's war trophies from public statues and in stopping any more demonstrations. Such measures will, he believes, lower the dictator's reputation in the city.

Commentary

This short introductory scene is typical of Shakespeare's use of minor incidents in his original. It serves several dramatic purposes:

1 Summarizes recent events and gives the date.
2 Reveals opposition to Caesar's growing power among officials of the republic.
3 Introduces the mob and its fickleness. Actually there was no great enthusiasm for Caesar: Shakespeare makes them turn out here to prepare the audience for the greater change of heart in Act III: this parallelism is one of his favourite devices.

The 'commoners', elsewhere 'plebeians' in a dangerous mood, are here seen in a holiday spirit. They are the same Elizabethan crowd that later forgives Caesar with all their hearts and cries 'Alas, good soul!' The cobbler's mock-logic is of the same stuff as the humour of the Grave-digger in *Hamlet* and the Porter in *Macbeth*.

In this and two other scenes (I,2 and III,2) the demarcation between verse and prose is clear-cut, the first being for passionate utterance and lofty expression, the second for poking fun or elaborating an argument. The audience does not notice the change to measured lines, but it senses the alteration in rhythm.

mechanical Craftsmen.

the sign . . . profession Not a badge or uniform, but simply their working clothes and the tools they carry.

rule Measuring rod.

in respect . . . workman Compared with a master-craftsman.

cobbler A mender of everyday shoes; also one who makes a clumsy attempt.

naughty Worthless.

out with Angry with.

out i.e. out at heels.

Thou art a cobbler Flavius, apparently the senior of the two tribunes, recognizes, unlike Marullus, that cobbling is a 'trade'.

awl A tool for making small holes, e.g. in leather.

withal Depending on the punctuation, this can mean either (1) nevertheless or (2) with all.

recover A pun on 'recover', to restore to health, and 're-cover', to repair (shoes).

neat's Cow's.

rejoice The key-word that spurs Marullus to unexpected eloquence.

tributaries Probably the hostages surrendered by defeated nations which have agreed to pay tribute.

You blocks, you stones . . . things In Antony's speech (III,2,144) this is what they are *not*!

blocks Blockheads, originally wooden blocks on which to place wigs and hats.

her banks The Tiber was normally a masculine river name.

replication Echoing.

concave shores Overhanging banks eroded by the current.

over Pompey's blood Caesar arrived in Egypt to find his rival had been assassinated. This triumph is to celebrate his defeat of Pompey's two sons in Spain, at the important battle of Munda.

intermit Stop.

most exalted Highest.

where Whether.

basest metal i.e. the very poor metal (mettle) of which they are made (lead easily melts).

Disrobe the images Remove from the statues any 'ceremonies', i.e. trophies, that may have been placed on them.

the feast of Lupercal It was the custom during the Lupercalia, held on February 15th, in honour of Pan, the shepherd god of fertility, for youths to run naked through the streets, whipping those they met with thongs of goat-skin. It would be characteristic of Antony (in Scene 2) to play a part so out of keeping with the diginity of consul and to take advantage of the festival spirit by trying 'how the people take' the half-playful crowning of Caesar.

the vulgar The common people.

These growing feathers . . . pitch A metaphor from the popular Elizabethan sport of falconry, and a puny blow at the great dictator, seen as a predator. However, the last two lines adequately prepare the audience for the pre-eminent position of the man who is about to enter on the stage.

Act I Scene 2

Caesar's first appearance is that of an absolute monarch, attended by a retinue of obsequious flatterers; yet very soon an impression of personal weakness in himself and of secret hostility towards him is conveyed to an audience who are aware of his ultimate fate.

First, like a king anxious to continue his dynasty, he calls on his chief supporter Antony to observe the primitive religious rite that may cause his wife to bear him an heir. Immediately after that, the shrill voice of a mysterious Soothsayer warns him against the ides of March (which will fall on the 15th of the month when the moon is full – significant to an Elizabethan audience).

When the procession has moved on, Cassius draws his friend Brutus aside to question him about their mutual estrangement. (In historical fact Caesar had awarded the praetorship to his favourite Brutus instead of to the more experienced Cassius.) When Brutus confesses that personal problems are the cause of his apparent unfriendliness, Cassius declares he will speak out what he has been keeping to himself. He informs Brutus that in these days of what he regards as oppressive government, many look to him for leadership.

Twice Cassius's long harangue is punctuated by cheers from the crowd at the ceremony off-stage – more significant when heard than when seen, especially as the applause is interpreted wrongly, so reinforcing Cassius' argument. He seizes on Brutus's fear that Caesar has been elected king, and feels his way to ever bolder utterance. After all, what's in the name of Caesar that makes him the only man in Rome that matters? There was a Brutus once (believed then to have been Brutus's ancestor, who expelled the last king of the Romans in 509 BC) who would not have tolerated a king (the hated word is out). Perhaps moved by this reference, Brutus pleads for a postponement of the discussion until a more convenient time, with the assurance that he would prefer obscurity to any office under a tyranny.

As the procession returns from the festival the two friends note an atmosphere of depression, as if something has gone wrong. In a conversation aside from the others we hear Caesar observe that Cassius has a sinister look. In spite of Antony's attempt at reassurance, he compares Cassius' personal attitudes (puritanical by the standards of Shakespeare's day) with Antony's own love of entertainment.

The two budding conspirators are left alone again, this time with Casca, at whose cloak Cassius has prompted Brutus to tug. This contemptuous aristocrat gives a caustic account of what has happened: Antony had offered Caesar a kind of crown, but to the great man's disappointment the enthusiasm of the crowd had increased with each reluctant refusal; in the end Caesar had fallen down in a fit – a spectacle portrayed by the cynical Casca much as it might have happened in the crowded Cheapside of Shakespeare's day. Cassius fails to make his point about Romans falling down in awe of Caesar. However, he invites Casca to dinner the following day (an engagement overtaken by events) and, after he has gone, explains to Brutus that Casca's mocking attitude disguises real determination.

In a closing soliloquy Cassius admits aloud that he has seduced Brutus from loyalty to his benefactor. This exposure of a reverse and less pleasant side to his character is an antecedent to that by Antony in *his* soliloquy (III, 1,260). He departs, taking on himself what so often falls to the lot of the devoted organizer, the production and distribution of literature!

Commentary

The effectiveness of this scene, which introduces all the principal characters, sketches in the political background and sets the stage for the main action, is enhanced by the alternation of public occasion and private conference. Also contrasted are loud proclamations with whispered hints, single cries with the distant roar of the multitude, the recollection of past episodes with the forecasting of future developments, hidden thought with frank utterances, superficial appearance (He's a 'dreamer', 'he's not dangerous', 'What a blunt fellow') with the underlying reality.

There is little prose in the play, most of it spoken here by Casca in his mood of 'foolery'. Providing some comic relief to Cassius's implacable earnestness, he is in the very next scene transformed into the awe-struck spectator of supernatural manifestations, which he describes in highly emotional verse.

Peace ho! Casca, afterwards the first to strike a blow, is here foremost among Caesar's adulators (cf. line 14); or is he already mocking at the foolery?

To touch Calphurnia Caesar's desire for an heir is an appropriate opening to a scene concerned with his pretensions to royalty.

our elders say The foremost intellect of his day covers his connivance at a superstitious belief by quoting tradition.

press Crowd.

Sennet The sound of a trumpet.

the trouble of my countenance The mental worry that my face would otherwise show.

Merely Wholly.

passions of some difference Conflicting emotions. Brutus has been anxious, before being approached by Cassius, about the threat to republican freedom by a man who has shown him great favour.

some soil . . . my behaviours Grounds for my attitude.

construe any further Take otherwise.

By means whereof . . . value i.e. until this explanation he has kept back ideas he would have liked to communicate to Brutus.

shadow Reflection (of your true self).

of the best respect Of the highest reputation.

had his eyes i.e. would only look (at his own reflection).

laugher Pope's emendation of Folio 'laughter', accepted by some as 'object of laughter'; an equally suitable substitution is 'lover'.

stale Cheapen.

scandal Slander.

profess myself in banqueting Make declarations of friendship after dining and wining.

rout A large party present on a social occasion.

Set honour . . . indifferently i.e. suggest any patriotic scheme involving both personal honour and the risk of death, and I will welcome them with equal readiness.

speed me as Prosper me proportionately as.

controversy Contesting (either with each other or the torrent). Caesar's challenge and humiliating failure are Shakespeare's invention.

Aeneas Legendary ancestor of the Romans, who carried his father from the sack of Troy and reached Italy after years of wandering.

from their colour fly i.e. turn pale. A pun on deserting military colours.

bend Look.

speeches The only reference to any of Caesar's many accomplishments.

Alas The pity is ironical.

Titinius He appears in person in IV,2.

new honours i.e. wearing a crown outside Italy.

narrow i.e. made to seem narrow by his standing astride of it.

Colossus A statue that, according to legend, bestrode the entrance to the harbour of Rhodes.

not in our stars Not due to an astrological destiny. Brutus makes a similar point in another well-known passage (IV,3,217).

Brutus and Caesar Appealing to the republican belief in equality.

sounded Uttered (with respect).

conjure with 'em Use them as magic words to summon up spirits. Brutus is to be visited by a 'spirit' without any invocation (IV,3,274).

start Cause to appear.

the great flood The Biblical disaster had a parallel in classical myth.

wide walls Emendation of Folio 'walks'. The width must refer to the distance between one side of the city and the other.

Rome and room Cassius's puns are bitter.

There was a Brutus once Lucius Junius Brutus expelled Tarquin, the tyrannical last king of Rome and became one of the first two consuls. He was famed for his republican zeal, executing two sons for their share in a royalist revolt.

As easily as a king Their assumption that Caesar has actually been crowned causes them some surprise at the embarrassment soon to be shown by Caesar's train.

nothing jealous Not at all in doubt.

villager Provincial without Roman citizenship.

pluck Casca Cassius knows his man.

The angry spot Brutus would be familiar with Caesar's changes of expression.

a chidden train Followers who have been severely rebuked.

conference Public debate.

scorn'd his spirit ... be mov'd Despised his own mind for being moved.

this ear is deaf Antony should be no stranger to Caesar's weaknesses, but this is Shakespeare's invention.

the rabblement shouted The folio 'howted' must be a mistake, as it indicates disapproval.

chopt Chapped (with hard work).

sweaty night-caps An aristocratic sneer at their rough head-coverings. Yet in Scene 1 they wore their 'best attire'.

I know not what ... that Caesar's epilepsy means something different to each of the three speakers: Brutus refers literally to the infirmity, Cassius uses it metaphorically for submission to tyranny, while Casca sticks to his narrative of Caesar's pathetic exhibitionism.

An(d) If.

if Caesar had stabb'd their mothers The mob was not so complacent after the stabbing of Caesar!

it was Greek to me i.e. 'double-Dutch'. Cicero is given a very minor part for one who was a learned orator and prominent statesman. In Plutarch Casca himself cried out in Greek during the assassination.

put to silence i.e. executed. In Plutarch they were merely deprived of office.

foolery Brutus's attitude to the dictatorship is one of patriotic misgivings, Cassius' of personal jealousy, Casca's of ribald disgust.

quick mettle Of an intelligent disposition.

tardy form i.e. pretended slowness in the uptake.

to digest his words Was there any special meaning behind Casca's account of Caesar's refusal of the crown?

wrought Worked upon (from the same root-word: cp. 'wrought-iron').

'tis meet . . . likes Cassius admits the wrong that he is doing to the character of Brutus.

He should not humour me He would not succeed in converting me to his opinion.

in several hands Written in different styles.

Act I Scene 3

The same night a violent storm has broken out, with unnatural incidents sufficiently frightening to change Casca's cynicism into terror. The burning hand of a slave, the men walking about in flames, the lion that declined to savage him, and the owl hooting in the Forum in broad daylight – these he regards as omens of something terrible, but they make little impact on the philosophic Cicero, who is less interested in messages from the gods than in the politically important question of whether Caesar will attend the meeting at the Capitol.

As Cicero departs, Cassius enters, his ear quick to recognize Casca's voice. Noting the impression made on his friend by the storm, he elaborates still further the nocturnal happenings and alters their significance from that of an *omen* to that of a *symbol* of the terrible times they are living in: monstrous night, monstrous dictator. His earlier bravado in tempting the lightning to strike him fails to rouse a response, but when Casca hesitantly guesses that the 'monster' is Caesar, he declares he will commit suicide sooner than exist under such tyranny. He goes on to blame the excessive power acquired by this otherwise quite ordinary man on the feeble resistance of contemporary Romans.

The two men clasp hands in agreement to seek a remedy for such a sad state of affairs, and Cassius reveals the formation of a band of conspirators, now awaiting for him in Pompey's Porch. A third shadowy figure, again swiftly identified by Cassius, proves to be one of the band, Cinna; his wish that Brutus could be made to join is immediately taken advantage of by Cassius, who hands him some of the papers to place where Brutus cannot but read them. The concluding remarks, on the reputation of Brutus and his potential value to the cause, are a link with that hero's next appearance.

Commentary

The storm – continued throughout the next act as a dark background to dark plottings – increases the sense of time elapsing between the Soothsayer's warning and the assassination. The descriptive speeches of Casca and Cassius, one apparently wondering why all the commotion, the other providing the answer, are more powerful in their effect than any noises-off the stage management can achieve. Shakespeare takes the events of that night as they were remembered afterwards and recorded by historians, including Plutarch, and uses them to heighten the tension. They are the terrible accompaniment of a terrible deed. The previous day's owl hooting in the Forum by daylight may seem insignificant recollected in present circumstances, but the Romans attached much importance to omens from birds. On the other hand, Casca's lion was borrowed by Shakespeare from the Tower of London!

Note the inconsistency between Cassius's previously declared familiarity with Casca's real outlook and trustworthiness and the prolonged bout of persuasion needed before Casca, 'tardy' as ever, finally commits himself. Perhaps it is just one more instance of Shakespeare's love of parallel events: Cassius' two efforts at winning over recruits. The relative importance of Caesar and Brutus in this play has often been discussed; what is sometimes overlooked is the nearly equal prominence throughout of Cassius. This is undoubtedly one of his scenes. Caesar, Brutus and Antony were trained rhetoricians; Cassius relies only on his passionate utterances.

brought you Caesar home? i.e. were you among his escort? Casca had been prominent in the ceremony. This linking question shows that Shakespeare has made the ides of March the day after the feast of Lupercal.

riv'd Riven (old word for split).

too saucy with Lacking due reverence for.

anything more wonderful Anything else more worthy of notice than this. This leading question marks off the natural wonders from the supernatural.

not sensible of Not feeling.

glaz'd Looked fixedly (as if without comprehension); 'glared' is unsuitable as the beast did not follow up by 'annoying' (doing harm to) him.

ghastly Pale with fear (cf. 'aghast').

market-place Elizabethan for Forum.

portentous things . . . point upon Omens to the region where they manifest themselves.

strange-disposed Ill-regulated.

Clean from the purpose . . . themselves Quite contrary to what is really intended.

A very pleasing night to honest men i.e. dark enough for the purposes of men who are on the right side.

Those that have known . . . faults i.e. those (who recognize the imminent celestial threat) also understand what is wrong in the world of men.

unbraced With loosened doublet.

thunder-stone Thunderbolt.

I did present myself Cassius made his appeal to Brutus an intellectual plea for freedom and equality, but his appeal to Casca is the desperate cry of one who prefers suicide to bondage.

astonish Stun (mentally): stronger than the modern sense of 'surprise'.

You are dull, Casca. This remark does not tally with his defence of Casca's 'bluntness' in the previous scene.

you do want Are lacking in you.

from quality and kind i.e. at variance with the normal behaviour of their species.

their ordinance Their ordained condition.

nature and pre-formed faculties Natural functions and the abilities they were originally endowed with. The tautology (needless repetition) here is in keeping with the repetitive 'why?'

monstrous quality Abnormal behaviour.

monstrous state Abnormal political condition (not mere repetition). Cassius finds in the storm an analogy for Caesar's 'tyranny'.

the lion in the Capitol Is this Casca's surly beast? The audience was familiar with the small embryo zoo kept at the Tower of London from the time of Henry III to 1834.

In personal action Cassius has in mind the frailties he pointed out to Brutus.

Let it be who it is In spite of his declared personal knowledge of Casca, he is not yet sure of him.

thews An archaic and rather general word, perhaps 'muscles'.

our fathers' minds i.e. the mental qualities we have inherited.

worldly bars i.e. human flesh.

know all the world Let all the world know.

That part . . . bear The tyranny as it affects me.

cancel With the double meaning of (1) repudiating a 'bond' (document) in his own handwriting, and (2) breaking his 'bonds' (chains). To Romans suicide was an accepted way out.

hinds Possibly another pun, on (1) female deer, which are timid, and (2) farm-hands, lacking spirit.

base matter i.e. the material in the bonfire.

illuminate Light up (not burn).

So vile a thing as Caesar! Is this a carefully calculated climax, like Antony's 'bloody treason' (III,2,194) or an uncontrollable outburst? 'Vile' means cheap or of poor quality.

My answer i.e. to a charge of treason.

arm'd Prepared to defend himself: again suspicious of the man he pretended to know.

fleering Grinning (as he tells the tale).

factious Seditious (inciting rebellion).

griefs Grievances.

undergo Undertake.

Of honourable-dangerous consequence Whose result will be either honour or death.

Pompey's porch A porch of a hundred marble columns extended in front of the great theatre built a few years previously by Pompey to hold thousands of spectators and hundreds of lions, a not inconsiderable factor in his popularity. This colonnade was a favourite resort by day; by night there would be dark corners in which 'honest men' could foregather.

no stir No movement.

complexion of the element Colour of the sky.

Who's that? The mistaking of Casca for Cimber emphasizes the surrounding darkness.

one incorporate One who has joined as a member (though only just).

Be you content i.e. don't worry. Cassius is confident that he has succeeded with Brutus.

the praetor's chair i.e. Brutus's, in the senate.

all this done Quite a feat in the circumstances!

hie Hasten.

yields him ours Surrenders to our persuasion.

countenance Approval.

conceited Expressed.

Revision questions on Act I

1 Write character sketches of Caesar (a) as he appears in Scene 2, and (b) as Cassius sees him.

2 Give as detailed an account as you can of what happened at the feast of the Lupercal.
3 Describe the state of Brutus's mind and indicate the parts of Cassius's speech he would find most persuasive.

Act II Scene 1

While Lucius, his young attendant, has gone to put a light in his 'study' in readiness for another night's reading, Brutus rehearses the leading argument he has been using to convince himself that Caesar, so recently his benefactor, must die: were the latter given supreme power as a king, his present reasonable behaviour would change to sheer tyranny. His ambition, therefore, has to be defeated before it has developed to extremes.

Lucius returns, bringing Brutus one of those anonymous letters written by Cassius and delivered by Cinna through the window. As he reads the typical message of incitement to 'save Rome' by striking now, a knock, at this late hour, is heard at the door. Before Lucius introduces the six conspirators, Brutus further soliloquizes on the loss of sleep he has suffered: the time now elapsing between the first suggestion of assassination and the moment of its performance is for him filled with a nightmarish emotional upheaval. Lucius informs his master that the visitors are so heavily masked that he cannot name them, a circumstance which leads to a personification by Brutus of 'Conspiracy' as an evil spirit lurking in dark places.

Having introduced the others one by one, Cassius draws Brutus aside (presumably to hear him declare his adherence) while the rest argue about the exact direction of the east, required for the swearing of the communal oath. Here Brutus makes his first break with Cassius in a long lecture on the undesirability of such a thing, their cause alone being sufficient to give them confidence in one another: their mere word as Romans should be unbreakable. When the name of Cicero is put forward (he is a prominent politician and enemy of Caesar, of whom we have had our only glimpse in the last scene) Brutus is quick to oppose the idea.

Brutus insists there should be no killing of Caesar's followers. Despite Cassius's protests, even Antony is to be spared. The killing must be by patriots performing a sacred rite, not by butchers wreaking indiscriminate vengeance (as was to happen when the Caesarians drew up their proscription). In fact it is a pity that the *spirit* of Caesar could not be destroyed without the shedding of blood. Antony is anyway a self-indulgent playboy and therefore harmless.

In response to doubts as to whether Caesar will attend the meeting at which they now design to kill him, *Decius* Brutus (another protégé of the dictator) claims he can flatter him into masking any superstitious fears. He will, in fact, escort him to the Capitol (chosen by Shakespeare as more likely to impress an audience than a 'court-house adjoining Pompey's porch'); they will all escort him, and Brutus fixes the time for them to call on him at the 'eighth hour'. As they depart Brutus gives Metellus a message for Ligarius.

After so much discussion the night has gone very quiet. Into this stillness steals Portia, who devotedly catechizes her husband about his night-walking and neglect of meals, demanding to know the reason. She may be a woman, but as his wife and Cato's daughter, she should be strong enough to keep a secret and has, in fact, inflicted a wound on herself as a test of her endurance. Brutus is overcome and promises to tell her all. Meanwhile Ligarius has answered Brutus's message in person by leaving his sick bed and calling on him. He is prepared to face the most impossible adventure, if Brutus is the leader.

Commentary

In contrast with the street scene, with its thunder and lightning and strange appearances round the corner, are the domestic interiors of the second Act. A conspicuous role is played by the two wives with difficult husbands, one of whom is honour-bound to keep a secret, the other all-powerful, but fearful of attempts on his life. Both wives kneel in petition (another Shakespearian 'double') but while Portia is alone with Brutus and able to prove her constancy, Calphurnia, though supported by the omens, is thwarted by the wily Decius (II,2), the nearest character in this play to a complete villain.

In Scene 1 two main themes have emerged: the ambition of Caesar and the honour of Brutus. Caesar must be killed, not for what he is now, but for what his ambition may lead to; the conspirators must follow Brutus's example and rely, not on a sworn oath, but on the honour of the whole band (though later it would seem that one of them must have leaked information to Artemidorus).

The three points on which Brutus forces Cassius to give way (no oath, the exclusion of Cicero, and the sparing of Antony) are as the successive stages of a conflicting relationship between the two men, leading up to more vital confrontations. In this scene a climax is reached when the normally 'sober' Brutus is moved to a passionate oration, with its repeated appeals: 'Let us be sacrificers . . . Let's carve him boldly'. He distinguishes between the ambitious *spirit* of Caesar and the *man* they all know.

Brutus's squeamishness over the spilling of blood is to contrast oddly with the almost fanatical request in III,1, 'let us bathe our hands in Caesar's blood/Up to the elbows.' Perhaps this play owes some of its success to the frequency with which several of its characters behave in inconsistent and contradictory fashion, albeit in minor connections. Conscious or unconscious on the part of the author, this dramatic approximation to 'reality' – a world often lacking in clear explanation and well-founded justification – may indeed be placed to Shakespeare's credit as much as to his often alleged carelessness.

Orchard Garden (not in Shakespeare's day limited to fruit-trees).
by the progress of the stars i.e. the storm has obscured them.
It must be by his death A clear-cut opening to the first of several self-revealing soliloquies. Brutus is prompt in making decisions: it is the following interval that he finds agonizing, with its problems of security and organization.
Get me a taper Put a candle.
spurn at Strike.
would be Wants to be.
that i.e. emphatically the last thing a Roman wants.
a sting Popular belief; an adder bites.
Remorse Pity (for others).
lowliness . . . ladder i.e. the ambitious man begins in a humble way at the lowest rung by ingratiating himself with the populace – as Caesar had done.
Looks in the clouds i.e. no longer downward.
prevent Anticipate, by acting first.
bear no colour . . . he is Have no justification in the light of his present character.
Fashion it thus Express our case in this way.
augmented i.e. with the addition of royal authority.
extremities Extremes.

serpent's egg Harking back to his original comparison. There is a certain artificiality about these analogies of the adder (Caesar) and the ladder (ambition), reflecting perhaps doubts about his own sincerity.

as his kind Because of its species; 'his' was eventually replaced by 'its' when referring to neutral objects.

calendar Recently reformed by his intended victim.

exhalations Meteors.

thou receivest Thy full petition Thou wilt have thy petition granted in full (provided redress is added to word and deed).

Since Cassius first did whet me . . . slept This implies several sleepless nights instead of one (and that the present one); cf. 'often dropp'd', used similarly of the letters (line 49). Shakespeare's telescoping of events was not always accompanied by minor adjustments.

motion Movement (in an undertaking). Brutus has interchanged beginning and end, as if he were looking back from the critical moment to the first stirrings, having experienced the agony of the intervening period.

phantasma Nightmare.

The genius . . . council A man's guardian spirit disputes with his impulses whether he is to think of his own safety or to act.

insurrection Upheaval.

your brother Cassius Cassius married Brutus's sister, Junia.

moe More.

the faction The party of agitators.

dangerous brow Face of one who is a threat.

evils are most free i.e. crime is more easily committed.

Hide it in smiles and affability Brutus's lofty scorn becomes practical advice in lines 224–7.

path, thy native semblance on Walk about looking as you really are.

Erebus The son of Chaos (in classical myth the empty space before creation). The name signifies darkness and was, therefore, as here, applied to the gloomy territory under the earth, through which the departed passed into Hades.

dim Dark.

prevention Being thwarted.

Decius Brutus Historically Decimus (Decius in Plutarch) was as important in the conspiracy as his namesake Marcus Brutus. He had been named next heir after Octavius.

Here lies the east The others, while their leaders confer, are preoccupied with a necessary preliminary to any Roman conspiracy – the swearing-in facing east.

fret Eat into, or decorate as with fretwork.

growing on the south Farther to the south. Inaccurate, as in mid-March the sunrise would be nearly due east.

Give me your hands . . . one i.e. instead of an oath. The hand-shaking in III,1,184 is a grim parallel to this testimony of one man's trust in another. Brutus has no sooner formally accepted leadership than he goes against the advice of Cassius.

the face of men . . . abuse i.e. the shame on men's faces, the sufferings in our own souls, the present wrongs (three strong motives that make an oath superfluous).

drop by lottery Meet his fate individually.

secret Romans Romans sharing a common secret.

palter Play false.

honesty to honesty An optimistic view of his fellow-conspirators.

fall for it i.e. perish in attempting redress.

cautelous Taking excessive precautions.

carrions i.e. no more use than corpses.

Is guilty of a several bastardy i.e. every drop becomes base blood, un-Roman.

his means Antony was Caesar's fellow-consul. Immediately after the assassination he fled to Caesar's house and took possession of his papers, including the will.

Our course will seem too bloody Brutus fondly believes the people will honour them for moderation.

like wrath in death . . . afterwards i.e. anger in the killing, followed by malice towards the corpse.

Let's be sacrificers, but not butchers He gives the attempt on the life of his friend and patron a sacred aspect.

And after seem to chide 'em Anger should cease when its object is attained. For this cooling-off, so characteristic of Brutus, cf. IV,3,111-2.

purgers Purifiers (of the state).

that were much he should He is hardly likely to do that. Actually Antony, when he sees Caesar's body, will offer his life: 'Fulfil your pleasure' (III,1,159). This remark typifies Brutus's fatal underestimation of Antony.

count the clock A celebrated Shakespearian anachronism. Roman water-clocks had no striking mechanism. The nocturnal effect of the stage-strokes as they listen to them increases the tension.

from the main opinion Contrary to his personal conviction. Cassius is himself to revert to superstition (V,1,78).

ceremonies Omens.

augurers Augurs were priestly interpreters of omens. This anticipates their report in the next scene.

unicorns The hunters of these fabulous animals were said to stand in front of trees and then side-step their victims.

toils Snares.

give his humour the true bent Put him in the right mood.

He loves me well, and I have given him reasons The usual relationship of Brutus with his friends: affectionate admiration on their part, philosophic lectures on his. Or it may mean, 'I have given him good reason (cause) to love me.'

put on our purposes Reveal our intentions. Ironical, in view of his own immediate self-betrayal by his looks when his wife enters.

formal constancy i.e. fidelity to the part being played.

Manet Remains. A Latin stage direction, like *exeunt*, they go out.

honey-heavy dew Metaphor for sleep that comes naturally, deep and refreshing.

figures Mental pictures.

weak condition Portia was delicate. Brutus does not yet know of her self-inflicted wound which (in Plutarch) produces a fever.

physical Curative.

unbraced With loosened doublet (Elizabethan).

the vile contagion . . . air i.e. the prevailing damp atmosphere, which causes rheumatism.

sick offence Cause of your illness.

my place i.e. as your wife.

charm Conjure.

that great vow Part of a Christian wedding.

Is it excepted Is there a clause making an exception?

in sort or limitation Limited to special provisions in the 'bond'.

suburbs Where (London) harlots were to be found.

Cato Marcus Cato Uticensis, 'whom Brutus studied most to follow of all the other Romans' (Plutarch). Father of the Cato in Act V and doubly related to Brutus, being brother of the latter's mother as well as father of his wife Portia. He was a keen republican and a Stoic, having committed suicide at Utica sooner than surrender to Caesar.

Think you I am no stronger than my sex Yet that very weakness is to be demonstrated in her (II,4,39).

charactery Writing (i.e. what is expressed there).

kerchief Cloth head-covering.

deriv'd from honourable loins i.e. descended from the earlier Brutus.

exorcist One who conjures up spirits, usually to drive them out of victims possessed by them.

mortified Dead. This invalid's exploit in rising instantly from his bed comes quickly after Portia's rebuke to her husband for exposing himself to the night air.

make sick Euphemism for 'slay'.

Act II Scene 2

For the first and only time we see Caesar alone; he refers briefly to the storm and his wife's nightmare, in which he is murdered. Saying little, but doubtless thinking much, he sends instructions for his augurs to perform a religious sacrifice and examine the victim for omens on the day's engagements. Calphurnia enters, terrified by the news of the supernatural manifestations. She does not refer to her own dream, perhaps because she feels that Caesar (who has already listened to her cries) would pay little attention to it, but she boldly (or frantically) forbids him to leave the house.

Caesar in boastful mood (unworthy of the man known to history), scorns fears of death, for it is inevitable; even when an unfavourable omen at the sacrifice is reported he declares he is more dangerous than any danger. After she has begged him on her knees to blame her fears for his non-attendance, he yields to please her; he will tell Antony, whom he is expecting at any moment, to explain to the assembly that he is not feeling well.

However, instead of his loving lieutenant, late up as usual, (see reference to the time below), there enters Decius, the decoy, and Caesar at once alters his excuse of illness to a flat refusal to attend (good enough for the old men of the Senate). He is angry with Calphurnia for intervening with the plea of sickness, and goes on to a detailed description of his wife's overnight vision of his 'statue' spouting blood, in which smiling Romans dipped their hands. Calphurnia has nothing further to say; the quick-witted Decius, faced with this phantasm of real human sacrifice (how and when Caesar was told about it we can only guess), thinks up an interpretation of the fountain as the source of Rome's revival. He reinforces this sample of the 'flattery' he knows so well how to apply to Caesar with the news that a crown (the first for several centuries) is to be offered to him. To stay at home would only lead to remarks unworthy of the dictator – for whom he professes his accustomed affection. Caesar decides to go, and the remainder of the band troop in, together with dear old Publius. They are followed by an Antony too surprised by so many early callers to utter more than a brief greeting to his master, who welcomes all his 'good friends' with effusive courtesy. Brutus lingers behind to comment sadly on this hypocritical display of false 'friendship'.

Commentary

In the first two scenes of this second act (classically the stage of 'involvement' leading up to the climax) all the main characters have been fully developed, with the exception of Antony, who has been absent until the last moment; yet we have an image, at second-hand and rather one-sided, of this unpredictable instrument of fate.

Two essential decisions for the unfolding of the tragedy are made: in Scene 1 Brutus decides to take part in the murder; in Scene 2 Caesar decides to go to the Capitol. The tone is mostly conversational, among friends, indoors; two flights of fantasy, both the work of a Brutus, startle us with their blood-suffused preconceptions of the actual spectacle: in Scene 1 the victim killed ritually on an altar; in Scene 2 the martyr in whose revitalizing blood the worshippers bless themselves. There is much bloodshed in Shakespeare, but nowhere else anything quite like these two images. The next act is reserved for great oratory.

Nevertheless, for an audience drawn to the theatre by the prospect of a famous assassination, there is much to appreciate and the suspense is mounting. As in an overture, we are treated to several themes: the importance of omens, liberation from tyranny, masked conspiracy, the keeping of dangerous secrets, the honour of a verbal pledge, the course followed by the ambitious, the meaning of friendship – all with an awesome back-drop of thunder and lightning and squadrons in the sky. Political giants prove to be a prey to superstitious fears in their home circles; we move on to the Capitol, with Caesar hiding his anxiety and his enemies hiding their intentions.

The 'eighth hour' would strictly be two in the afternoon, as the Romans counted the hours from 6 a.m. That we are up early with the Elizabethans is clear from Caesar's remark to Brutus on his early stirring, and the appearance of Antony, having risen late from his bed. It was three in the early morning when the conspirators had left Brutus.

night-gown Dressing-gown.
Nor heaven nor earth There is an interesting contrast here with Brutus's opening words in the previous scene: for the calm Brutus the storm merely obscures the stars, while Caesar is appalled by its violence. Brutus has to shout to waken Lucius, but Caesar has had to listen to his wife's nightmare cries; Lucius is sent to put a light in the study, whereas Caesar's servant is despatched to order an animal sacrifice.
N'er look'd but on my back i.e. stood their ground only when I was looking the other way.
stood on ceremonies Relied on omens.
one within Stage expression for someone outside and at hand. The following 'who' is omitted.
the watch Strictly used of London's body of night watchmen.
fought This seems a necessary emendation of the Folio 'fight', but the latter might be the 'historic present' as spoken by the eye-witness; it is also transitional between the present perfect of 'have yawn'd' and the descriptive past tense of 'drizzled'.

hurtled Made clashing metallic sounds.

beyond all use Quite contrary to custom.

most strange An arrogant assertion that even a Stoic would not utter.

offering Usually a fowl.

in shame of cowardice To put cowardice to shame.

more dangerous . . . more terrible Unconscious irony, as this aspect of the dictator is the very cause of the plot against him. Note that his *name* is employed four times in these few lines.

for thy humour To relieve your anxious mood.

in very happy time At the appropriate moment.

I will not come to-day Again a fourfold repetition, giving the impression of a weak mind striving to be firm.

Say he is sick Calphurnia slips up in her urgency, is rebuked, and after this has nothing further to say.

stays Keeps.

She dreamt tonight This vision, not previously mentioned by Caesar or his wife, is Shakespeare's invention, possibly suggested by Plutarch's reference to the blood spattered on Pompey's statue. Tonight means the night which is nearly over.

like a fountain Had Shakespeare in mind a contemporary fountain in Cheapside, spouting wine on special occasions?

pure blood i.e. not diluted, as wine might be with water.

portents Omens.

For tinctures . . . cognizance Probably Decius is not too clear what he means. The first three words might apply, strangely enough, to the blood and bones of a martyr, the last means some kind of memento taken from the dead. None of them is appropriate to a fountain.

mock Apt to be render'd A likely mocking reply.

your proceeding Your affairs.

liable Legally subject i.e. good reasons must support what my affection requires me to say.

'tis strucken eight i.e. it is time to go. Brutus is impatient of the 'interim' (II,1,64). These are striking clocks in both houses! (An anachronism, as already pointed out.)

prepare within i.e. provide some wine before the procession sets off for the Capitol. This would seem the most suitable moment for Calphurnia's exit.

like friends i.e. all friends together. Trebonius's word is unconsciously echoed in Caesar's rather forced geniality, characteristic of the great man when among associates, and so different from his pompousness in public.

every like i.e. every superficial similarity (concealing real differences).

earns Yearns, grieves.

Act II Scene 3

Artemidorus reads aloud his comprehensive warning, naming all the conspirators. It is written on a paper he intends to hand personally to Caesar as if it were an ordinary petition. As his school of rhetoric was attended by some of Brutus's circle, there may have been a 'leak' or several 'leaks', but not necessarily deliberate ones.

Commentary

Dynamite to the conspiracy, this provides the audience with good reason for Portia's anxiety in the next scene.

immortal One of the flattering epithets often prefixed to Caesar's name.
security gives way to conspiracy i.e. self-confidence provides an opportunity for a secret attack.
Out of the teeth of emulation Safe from assault by the envious.
contrive Conspire.

Act II Scene 4

Portia, now fully informed of the plot, is distracted with fear; she so lacks 'constancy' that she bids Lucius go to the Capitol merely to see how Brutus looks and note what men press their petitions on Caesar. She even thinks she detects the sound of fighting. The Soothsayer is an unfortunate person for her to question: his fears only serve to increase hers. We know now the reason for his prophetic warning: there is harm in store for Caesar, and he means to speak to him.

Confessing her feminine weakness, Portia expresses aloud a wish for the success of the enterprise; then, fearing that Lucius, still at her side, has overheard it, adds the explanation that Brutus is to make a request that will probably be refused – hence her anxiety! Finally she despatches the boy with a trifling message to her husband – that she is 'merry', the very word that Brutus used for hiding one's real feelings! Whether the boy saw the combined assault on one unarmed man, in which his master's sword rose and fell, is of no moment to the play. Probably Lucius thought of little beyond his round of duties and of snatching rest when he could.

Commentary

This scene not only fills the interval between Caesar's departure from his house and his arrival at the Capitol, but is a fine piece of characterization, created from hints in Plutarch.

Senate House There was no special building; the Senate met in various places. For this meeting, see note in Act III.

O constancy This quality of steadiness is now personified as a spirit summoned to her aid.

rumour Distant noise.

fray Affray, fighting.

Which way hast thou been? Wondering if he has been near the Capitol.

some suit to Caesar She is thinking of a written not an oral petition: she has not recognized the man who confronted Caesar the day before.

praetors Judges in civil law. Brutus and Cassius were among them.

void Empty of people.

Revision questions on Act II

1 How does Brutus justify to himself the murder of Caesar?

2 List, with explanations, Brutus's errors of judgement in this Act.

3 What argument does Portia use to try to persuade her husband to share her secret with her?

4 Analyse Caesar's reactions to omens and predictions.

Act III Scene 1

On the way to the Capitol Caesar challenges the Soothsayer over his warning and is reminded that the day is not yet finished. Artemidorus takes advantage of this pause in the procession to present his petition (which he calls a 'schedule', or formal proposal of public interest), but is cunningly thwarted by Decius, who brandishes a rival petition from Trebonius. When the desperate Artemidorus cries out that it closely concerns Caesar himself, the dictator seals his own fate by proudly putting it aside as of least importance. Cassius, with bitter sarcasm, calls on petitioners to make their respective cases at the meeting of the Senate, knowing full well how one suit is to be massively prosecuted.

After Caesar has taken his seat, Popilius Lena whispers his sympathy with their 'enterprise' and then goes straight to Caesar. This creates a moment of tension, but there is no sign of alarm and the conspirators proceed with their plan. Immediately Caesar has opened the proceedings in words befitting an absolute monarch, Metellus Cimber kneels before him; his petition (for the repeal of his brother's banishment) is quickly anticipated by Caesar and rejected with the contemptuous addition that those fawning for favours deserve the treatment meted out to curs.

Caesar's judgement is infallible. The whole pack then close in round him, crouching apparently in supplication, as he waxes eloquent on his constancy to what has been decreed by the state, a constancy that distinguishes him from the rest of shifting humanity. They might as well try to push Mount Olympus from its foundations! Is not Brutus (the one he would listen to most) pleading in vain? Then Casca, turning from words to action, gives the signal with an ineffectual first thrust (daunted no doubt by the personality of his victim). All stab Caesar in turn and when he see Brutus also ready to use his weapon on him, Caesar ceases to resist and falls at the base of the statue of Pompey, his once great rival.

In spite of Brutus's appeal to them to stay, the stunned spectators all flee the scene. Trebonius arrives to report general panic in the city, and Antony (whom he had detained in conversation) has fled to his house. Left to themselves the conspirators, led by Brutus: (1) consider they have saved Caesar twenty years of 'fearing death', (2) mark themselves with his blood as a badge of the freedom they have gained and (3) imagine their parts as liberators being acted in future stage plays! They are preparing to seek public support in the streets when Antony's servant enters to make a carefully rehearsed speech directed at Brutus and offering his master's co-operation if the killing of Caesar can be justified. In spite of Cassius's fears Brutus invites Antony to meet them.

Antony makes one of the most dramatic entrances in Shakespeare; he greets the dead conqueror first, before turning to the murders to declare he is prepared to die also at their hands. Brutus maintains that their cruel act was committed out of pity for Rome and offers friendship, followed up quickly by Cassius's more practical promise of political advantage. Antony then, astoundingly, shakes the hand of each in turn and, as if in compensation, utters an ironic and even poetical elegy over his stricken leader, interrupted by the impatient Cassius demanding to know which side he is on. Antony repeats that all he expects is good reasons – and, naturally, permission to speak at the funeral. Cassius's whispered objection is overruled by Brutus, who sets certain conditions: Antony must (1) not blame the killers, (2) enlarge on Caesar's good points, (3) publicly acknowledge that he speaks by permission, and (4) speak after Brutus.

Left alone with the body, dismissed by Brutus as 'no worthier than the dust', Antony addresses it passionately as 'thou bleeding piece of earth'; he pronounces a full-blooded curse, prophesying a brutal civil war. A servant of Octavius reports that Caesar's heir is close to Rome; Antony sends him a warning to keep clear till he has tested the feelings of the populace in a speech.

Commentary

The assassination is the climax: it has been plotted in the first two acts and will be avenged in the last two. It is a celebrated historical fact, and something the audience has looked forward to most of all (this blood-thirsty feature of English stage productions was regarded as a fault by classical dramatists on the continent, who contrived that killings took place out of sight). Antony's speech in the next scene has been claimed as Climax Number Two, but among other reasons against this construction is the symmetrical one: the vital choice of the people after the murder balances the vital decisions before it.

The entry of Antony's servant could be called the 'turning-point'. The terrible blow for freedom has been struck, and now the liberators are uncertain of their immediate policy, whether to prepare to defend themselves or boldly proclaim their crusade from the rostrum outside. There is even some philosophizing on the benefits of being cut off in the prime of life (should events take a wrong turn). From this state of inaction Brutus rescues them with his almost sacramental proposal that they smear their arms and weapons with the dead man's blood, in order to wave them aloft before the public gaze, as a red sign of their emancipation from slavery.

The two scenes are outstanding examples of Shakespeare's stagecraft and command of language, the latter as uttered by Antony, the pleasure-loving soldier of genius. No less notable is the build-up of an autocratic Caesar, who behaves as if he were indeed the sovereign of his thwarted ambition. His manner is peremptory, his decisions irrevocable, and his wisdom infallible. His constancy is as immovable as Brutus's honesty is unshakeable. His decisions are *his*, much as the Senate is *his*. Thus a world figure of military and political genius appears as a tyrant whose vanity and arrogance are progressively unbearable. But it lessens the shock of the shambles that deprived the Roman state of its greatest representative. It is easier to watch the knifing of one who regards the Senate as his lackeys, treats humble petitioners as curs to be kicked out of the way, and is 'unique' in sticking to his decisions – less because they are decisions of state than because *he* made them.

the Capitol The name given to the Temple of Jupiter, chief building on the Capitoline Hill, most important of the Seven Hills of ancient Rome. The Senate met in various places, sometimes in the 'Capitol'. On this day it had been summoned (by Caesar) to meet at the Curia (hall of assembly) adjoining Pompey's Porch, but Shakespeare preferred the Capitol and moved Pompey's statue there as well.

Trebonius doth desire you . . . suit Is Decius aware of the threat from Artemidorus? Trebonius is unable to present the petition himself because he has been detailed to draw Antony away.

us ourself Note the royal first person plural.

read it instantly According to Plutarch, Caesar took the paper, but held it unopened.

your enterprise to-day The timing is enough to make Cassius fear discovery.

Casca, be sudden His first stroke is to be the signal for the general assault.

I will slay myself i.e. if Caesar escapes our attack.

presently At once.

puissant Archaic for 'powerful', used in addresses to monarchs.

prevent Anticipate.

These couchings This stooping low.

turn pre-ordinance . . . children Make what has been ordained and decreed (note the tautology) from the first days of creation into childish games with their changeable rules.

fond So foolish.

rebel i.e. rebelling against first decision.

thaw'd from the true quality . . . fools Seduced from holding to set standards by that which converts fools to softer attitudes.

nor without cause . . . satisfied i.e. he must be given good reasons why his actions should be condemned as unjustified.

Publius Cimber Not in Plutarch. The use of the name Publius in the play is confusing.

As low as to thy foot Ignoring Caesar's scorn for those who 'couch low'.

enfranchisement Re-admission to citizenship.

If I could pray to move i.e. if there were any higher authority than myself that could be moved by *my* prayers.

constant Steady.

whose true-fix'd . . . quality Whose precise location and reliability not to change.

no fellow in the firmament No equal in the sky. In its sense of 'a solid structure' this is an appropriate word here.

hold his place Remain in the same position (while other stars revolve).

apprehensive Able to reason or imagine. This line is parallel to 1.64:

'flesh and blood' corresponds to 'fire' and 'apprehensive' to 'shine'.

That unassailable . . . motion Who, because he is immune to attack, keeps his position and is not thrown off his course. Note the dramatic irony of 'unassailable'.

Let me a little show it i.e. allow me to prove it, even in such a minor matter as this.

Olympus Of several mountains in the Near East bearing this name, a lofty one in Greece (nearly 10,000 ft) was regarded as the abode of the gods. This extraordinary analogy is an attempt to make the efforts of his petitioners seem puny.

bootless In vain.

Et tu, Brute? You, too, Brutus? This is the Latin vocative case of address, 'O Brutus!' Not found in Plutarch, but Shakespeare had 'a little Latin'.

pulpits Public platforms. Shakespeare would be thinking of the famous 'pulpit' in St Paul's Churchyard, London.

confounded with this mutiny Confused by this insurrection.

Talk not of standing i.e. no posture of defence.

good cheer Don't be downcast.

abide Be responsible for.

drawing days out Prolonging their lives.

stand upon Think about.

twenty years Another 'score'? Caesar was 56.

His time of fearing death Cf. II,2,32 for Caesar's reference to such cowards.

bleed in sport i.e. be killed in a play.

on Pompey's basis i.e. the base of his statue.

knot of us Our tightly knit group.

grace his heels Follow close behind.

being prostrate More lowly crouching!

be resolv'd Have it explained. Cf. III,2,183.

thorough Through.

this untrod state These new conditions.

still Falls shrewdly to the purpose Still holds good.

let blood i.e. killed.

rank Overgrown (too big).

bear . . . hard Have a spite against.

purpled With red blood.

mean of death Method of execution.

by . . . by Beside . . . at your hands.

The choice and master spirits of this age The first example of Antony's irony.

see you but You see only.

so pity pity i.e. pity for Rome has driven out pity for Caesar.

in strength of malice Strong in their hostility. Referring again to the blood on their hands (1.167).

brothers' temper Brutus speaks for himself.

valiant Casca Sarcastic? If so, how did Antony find out in this short time that Casca had struck from behind? Cf. V,1,43.

not least in love This to the man who had enticed him away from the scene so that he could not take Caesar's part!

bay'd Brought 'to bay', like a stag.

sign'd in thy spoil . . . lethe Stained by your life-blood (the meaning of both phrases); 'spoil' applied to the dead body of a hunted animal, while Lethe was a river of the underworld which souls of the dead drank from to obtain oblivion.

the heart of thee i.e. this corpse was once the centre of the world. The pun was suggested by 'hart' in line 204.

prick'd in number of Marked down as one of.

Therefore i.e. in order to join you.

moreover The bombshell is introduced as an afterthought.

by leave and permission Tautology, for emphasis, as in lines 38,241, 255 and 263.

fall Happen (befall).

speak all good A loop-hole of which Antony is to make good use.

in the tide of times Not clear, 'tide' usually referring to a season or the ebb and flow of the sea, 'time' to a particular period concerned with particular human events (cf. Christmastide and Christmastime); perhaps 'in all the years that have come and gone'.

A curse shall light . . . men i.e. other limbs than Caesar's shall be mangled.

Até Greek goddess of evil deeds and blood revenge.

havoc No quarter.

carrion men . . . burial Dead men whose flesh is putrefying and who are 'crying out' to be buried (as if they were still alive, though wounded).

Rome of safety i.e. safe place (pun on Rome and room).

issue Handiwork.

Act III Scene 2

The Senate have vanished; it is the people who demand satisfaction (Caesar supported the popular party). The two leading assassins address the plebeians in separate assemblies. We listen to Brutus in an atmosphere of cautious respect. Using what is to us a curiously artificial rhetoric (see the notes on this speech) he begins by asking his hearers to listen carefully, trust his word and judge his cause sensibly. His love for Caesar was equal to that of anyone in his audience, but his love for Rome was greater. The alternatives were slavery under Caesar or freedom after his death. In a mounting climax he sheds tears for the man he loved, rejoices in his triumphs, honours him for his valour – but finds him deserving of death for his ambition. When he challenges anybody to find fault with him in the guise of (1) a slave, (2) a non-Roman, (3) a Rome-hater, there is, understandably, no reply.

The body of Caesar, with Antony as sole mourner, is brought in on a bier and covered with his mantle; Brutus recommends them to listen in turn to Antony and not follow him as he leaves the Forum (for the Capitol). Facing a crowd that has apparently been won over by Brutus ('Let him be Caesar', with a crown, a statue and a triumph), Antony begins cautiously and feels his way at every stage.

He disproves Caesar's ambition, but the 'honourable men' must be believed. (Doubts). He and they loved the great man, but the honourable men must not be wronged; there is a will, but to read it would anger the people against the honourable men. (The people approve the reading of the will; they crowd round him; he is one of them). He vividly imagines the assassination. (Tears). He shows them the victim – of *treason*. (Grief and rage). But they must not mutiny, because there are reasons; he does not wish to incite them; he is only letting the wounds speak for themselves; but if an orator like *Brutus* . . . (Mutiny). He calls them back to hear the will; there is a bequest for each of them. (Revenge). There is a bequest also to the city. (Riots).

Now let it work. Mischief, thou art afoot,
Take thou what course thou wilt! (III, 2,261–2)

Immediately and with cynical brevity Antony turns his moving speech morally inside out: it has been the *tour de force* of a political gambler. As a servant announces the actual (and on Antony's part the none too welcome) arrival of Octavius in Rome, and the flight of Brutus and Cassius, fortune is indeed 'merry' (III, 2,268).

Commentary

This scene is remarkable in that the speeches and their effects are as dramatic as the assassination itself. In Scene 1 the chances of the plot's being discovered provide tension; here tension is created by the changing responses of the mob of plebeians. The two speeches (which are public addresses) contrast sharply: Brutus's has the prose rhythm of the academic orator, Antony's the verse rhythm suited to a mass audience, rousing the emotions with its imagination, pathos, irony and hatred. Brutus argues down to the people, Antony identifies himself with them. Brutus explains the honourable character of his action, Antony mourns his friend, *their* friend.

Caesar's achievements and benefactions are good arguments and his will an irresistible weapon, cunningly wielded. Material benefits come home more surely than the call to freedom. It is when the body, with its twenty-three wounds, is uncovered, that the crowd begins to get out of hand. The sight of their mangled favourite makes them even forget the existence of the will. Caesar's dead body drives Brutus and his associates out of Rome to meet his spirit at Philippi. For the first and perhaps only time a funeral oration has changed the destiny of a nation.

part the numbers i.e. lessen the size of the crowd by division.

As Caesar loved me . . . I slew him Here the climax – weep, rejoice, honour – leads directly to an anticlimax – slew.

There is tears . . . ambition This repeats, in a second climax, the same ideas in the form of nouns instead of verbs – tears, joy, honour and (anticlimax) death.

Who is here so base . . . offended? By now his audience is attuned to this triplication. He reduces them to respectful silence by three rhetorical questions (with identical refrains), to answer any of which is to admit to being a slave, unRoman or a hater of Rome.

enroll'd in the Capitol i.e. entered in the records at a meeting held in the Capitol, an impossibility in Shakespeare's time schedule. The real conspirators made their way to the Capitol and addressed their fellow citizens there, and another day was to elapse before the funeral.

extenuated Lessened.

enforc'd Overemphasized.

Caesar's better parts . . . Brutus i.e. the greatness that was Caesar's shall live on in the sovereignty of Brutus. This exquisite irony was contrived by Shakespeare out of the comment of Plutarch that the crowd wanted Brutus to rule them.

grace Honour.

I come to bury Caesar . . . bones These famous lines might be paraphrased thus; 'Caesar will be remembered for his bad ambition, which caused him to be assassinated; he had good qualities, however, and these I mean to touch on before they are buried with him for ever.' The Romans practised cremation.

Caesar was ambitious Antony must have overheard this part of Brutus's speech (line 29) just before he entered this part of the Forum.

I thrice presented him This is the only one of the four points at all relevant to ambition, but all appealed to the popular mind.

O judgment! Seeing that he has the crowd with him, Antony lets himself go.

in the coffin Anachronism. Caesar's wounds would be more readily visible on a Roman bier.

there will a worse come in his place His rule will be succeeded by something worse.

abide it Pay dearly for it. Cf. III,1,94.

none so poor Antony is the only official mourner.

napkins An early Christian practice. In Caesar's case there must have been little blood left!

issue Descendants.

You are not wood . . . stones They had been called just that for forsaking Pompey for Caesar (I,1,35).

o'ershot myself i.e. gone too far (from an arrow passing beyond the target).

honourable men By 1.153 the irony is patent to the meanest intellect.

the Nervii A warlike tribe of the Belgae in northern Gaul. The victory, snatched out of imminent defeat, was celebrated by a long 'holiday', which the crowd would be likely to remember.

in this place These holes are a superb piece of make believe, as Antony was not even an eyewitness.

resolv'd Informed.

most unkindest The best-known example of a double superlative.

Ingratitude i.e. Brutus's lack of gratitude for favours received.

Which all the while ran blood 'Which ran all of a goare bloud *till he was slaine*' (Plutarch). This tradition of a statue spouting blood like a fountain probably suggested Calphurnia's dream (II,2); an account of it must have been related to Antony some time after the murder. It would also explain the lavish smearing of themselves by the conspirators.

honourable The word falls now on their ears with the force of hammer blows.

I only speak right on But Antony's speech is as cunningly developed as Brutus's was elaborately logical.

drachmas Greek silver coins circulating in the Roman sphere.

orchards See note p.33.

Mischief, thou art afoot Probably spoken with the goddess Até in mind (III,1,271).

upon a wish In answer to my unspoken wish.

Are rid Have ridden.

some notice of the people i.e. some signs of disturbance or shouting.

Act III Scene 3

An innocent poet Cinna, and friend of Caesar (Plutarch), whose name unfortunately for him coincides with that of one of the more conspicuous assassins, is mobbed to death. The crowd's first question demands his name, but in the confusion of his being interrogated in the same breath by the whole group, it is left to the last.

Commentary

Here is a minor tragedy to parallel the main one. This short scene: (1) shows the unreasonableness of the mob, (2) creates a gap in time between the funeral and the proscription and (3) adds a little much-needed comic relief. The historical Cinna made himself very unpopular by an anti-Caesar speech.

turn him going Send him away.

Revision questions on Act III

1 What have you noticed about Brutus's attitude to Caesar alive, Caesar dead, Antony, the Citizens?
2 Trace as exactly as you can, without drawing on the speeches, the course of events from the Soothsayer's reply to the arrival of Octavius.
3 Attempt a character sketch of the Fourth Citizen, based on his remarks in Scenes 2 and 3.
4 By a close look at Antony's speeches, show how he wins over the ordinary people in Act III Scene 2.

Act IV Scene 1

The 'butchers' have taken over from the 'sacrificers'. This terrible proscription, possibly in vengeance on those whom Caesar had spared only for them to kill him, but certainly to eliminate opposition, kept increasing in number. After a brief trading in lives, the unpleasant side of Antony's character is shown further by his treatment of Lepidus, who played a much more important part in events and who once rescued Antony from a desperate situation. In fact, he remained in charge in Rome while the other two campaigned against the republicans.

Octavius calls on Lepidus to agree to his brother's being put to death (as in all civil wars, families were divided in their allegiances); in return Lepidus requires sentence on Antony's nephew. As if in retaliation Antony requests Lepidus to fetch Caesar's will from Caesar's house. Here discrepancies appear: in III,2,266 Antony was to join the others at Caesar's house, not Antony's (was this errand an excuse to make Lepidus look like a beast of burden?); whichever house they could be meeting in, the will had already been read by Antony (was he the sort of man to part with it?).

Commentary

Why a full-length portrait should be made of a Triumvir who utters a few words and does not appear again is something of a mystery. There may, indeed, have been a contemporary figure whose 'accent yet unknown' would be familiar to the dramatist and the audience. No mention is made of Cicero, who was Octavius's contribution: perhaps Shakespeare thought that for Octavius to yield to Antony would be out of keeping with his obstinate character in the play. He asserts himself here as Antony's equal, though only nineteen, the son of Caesar's niece.

The reference to the will makes this scene follow naturally on the last, though the actual gap was eighteen months of highly complicated developments, and the meeting was in North Italy.

The indirect brutality of this episode invites comparison with the senseless mugging of poor Cinna.

damn Condemn.
cut off some charges in legacies Save expenditure.
To ease . . . loads To save ourselves from slanderous accusations of seizing too much for ourselves.
business i.e. the financial burden which is really ours.
empty ass Unladen donkey. The comparison is now explicit.
in commons On public pasture.
wind Turn.
His corporal motion . . . spirit His bodily movements controlled by my will.
taste Degree.
objects, arts Things of former popular interest (and now out of date), creations (now out of fashion).
imitations Fakes.
property Piece of furniture.
levying powers Raising armies.
Our best friends made . . . stretch'd Our friends enlisted on our side and our resources fully exploited.
How covert matters . . . disclos'd How to find out hidden snags.
at the stake Metaphor from bear-baiting.

Act IV Scene 2

Brutus and Cassius meet after what is in history a long interval, in which they have been raising forces in separate provinces. They were fortunate in enlisting large numbers of Pompey's discharged soldiers and some dissatisfied Asiatic princes, but there is no word of this in the play. The two armies have converged at Sardis, capital of Lydia, in Asia Minor, whence they will cross the Aegean Sea to northern Greece to meet the advancing troops of Antony and Caesar. There is some confusion in the stage direction: Lucilius is obviously returning from a visit to Cassius (line 3) accompanied by Cassius's slave, Pindarus; Lucius, not Lucilius, is with Brutus. Titinius, who is not spoken to until the last line of the scene, may be with Brutus as Cassius's representative, but, as Brutus's criticism of Cassius is addressed to the *slave* Pindarus, it is better to assume that he arrives *with* Cassius, instead of having what would be a double insult inflicted on him.

When Pindarus leaves (to rejoin Cassius) Brutus asks for and gets from Lucilius an account of the cooling relationship between the two leaders. The clash is immediate, and Brutus hastily suggests a private conference, to avoid damaging the troops' morale by the sight of their leaders quarrelling. Lucilius and Titinius guard the entrance to Brutus's tent.

Commentary

This scene, which some would make continuous with the next, prepares the audience for a bitter quarrel between two brothers-in-arms (and by marriage). Affection is strong for one another, as strong as the divisions, though at this stage it is not Brutus's errors of judgement that cause the trouble, but his lofty principles. The sad truth is that the man who cannot wait to accuse openly his friend of extortion is chronicled as having himself squeezed wealthy Asians for money, much of which was spent on a fleet, that, too late, won a victory.

He greets me well This must be a comment on a missive handed to Brutus by Pindarus.
In his own change In a change of attitude brought about by himself.
ill officers Officers exerting evil influences.
worthy cause Substantial reason.
He is not doubted There is no question about his honour.
familiar instances Signs of close friendship.
enforced ceremony Show of politeness.
hollow men Men of no substance or capacity to endure.
hot at hand Eager when curbed by the rein.
endure the bloody spur Be spurred into action.
fall their crests Let droop their neck ridges.

jades Horses of poor quality, hacks.

Stand! Passed from unit to unit off stage, this conveys the impression of a large army.

Wrong I mine enemies? An echo of 'Caesar doth not wrong' (III,1,47). According to Plutarch, on some occasions Brutus refrained from exacting ransoms from his prisoners.

content Quiet.

I do know you well i.e. your easily roused temper.

enlarge Give a full account of.

Lucius, do you the like The Folio (Lucilius) must be wrong, the names of Lucius (line 50) and Lucilius (1.52) being interchanged: they could have been easily confused in the printing. It is more appropriate for Lucius to take a message, similar to that of his fellow-attendant, Pindarus (1.47). Then Lucilius would be on guard with his fellow-officer Titinius, as he is when the 'poet' thrusts his way in (IV,3,123). Lucius would naturally return and be in attendance.

Act IV Scene 3

Cassius begins by reproaching Brutus for prosecuting one of his officers for taking bribes from the local inhabitants and also of paying scant attention to one of his supporting letters. Brutus in reply simply points to Cassius's own reputation for selling offices; this charge makes Cassius openly threaten his friend, but he is merely reminded that Caesar was slain for condoning such actions. Then Cassius protests that he is more experienced in such matters, and heated exchanges follow, Cassius gesticulating and Brutus smoothly retorting that he will not be intimidated by such angry outbursts. After a silly squabble over the use of 'elder', which might be taken to mean 'better', Cassius warns Brutus not to provoke him too far. Undeterred by the implied menace, Brutus specifies his charge in clearer but incompatible terms: Cassius has denied him a loan when he, Brutus, was unable to raise the necessary money by the means practised by Cassius. In vain Cassius explains there was a misunderstanding, for Brutus goes on to declare that such faults cannot be overlooked in a friend. Calling down vengeance (for their actions) on his head only, Cassius offers his dagger to Brutus and invites him to take his heart instead of the gold he has refused to give.

This gesture leads to their affectionate reconciliation, interrupted by a crazy cynic (styled a 'poet' by Shakespeare because he quotes two lines from Homer), a relaxation of tension, giving the audience, rather than the two protagonists, something to laugh at. They summon a conference, but before it begins Brutus breaks the news of Portia's death, which must, Cassius realizes, have been on his friend's mind during the argument. Portia's death seems to affect Cassius more deeply than it does her Stoic husband.

The conference reveals that Antony and Octavius are leading a large army into Greece and that there has been a proscription by them of about a hundred Senators believed to sympathize with the Republicans. His private grief is again broken, very gently, to Brutus and received by the bereaved with the same stoic brevity, 'Why, farewell, Portia.'

Brutus quickly turns to the military situation and recommends marching to meet the Caesarians at Philippi, a key position in Macedonia. Cassius once more loses the argument (he would hold back), worsted by the celebrated advice that must have propelled many doubters into prompt if not always successful action:

There is a tide in the affairs of men,
Which, taken at the flood, leads on to fortune. (IV, 2,217–18)

When his friends have gone, Brutus prepares for his usual night-reading, calls on Lucius for some music and tells his two attendants to lie down and sleep inside his tent. He tenderly takes the instrument from a Lucius too exhausted to play properly, and picks up his 'book' – then suddenly the taper flickers as a frightful apparition stalks in. It is Caesar's ghost, come to warn him that he will meet him again, at Philippi, Brutus's chosen battleground. When woken by Brutus the sleepers in the tent declare they have seen nothing, which is hardly surprising.

Commentary

In this scene the incompatibility of temperament between the two leaders evident throughout the play reaches its climax. Lofty motive confronts practical expediency. The quarrel is dramatic, not only in its stark character contrasts but in that it threatens to disrupt the republican forces, or at least demoralize the troops; on the other hand the reconciliation dignifies the two men just before their final farewell.

The portrait of Brutus is at full length: his idealism and the moral scruples that lead him into contradiction; his rigid philosophy with its display of well-considered reasons and its stoic indifference to grief; his devotion to books and music and his intolerance of moral or intellectual inferiority. There is also his gentleness and consideration for others; his calm temperament ruffled by one of those rare outbursts that are soon over, yet quite unruffled by a ghost; and, finally, the confidence in his own judgment that produces the last fatal blunder.

In Plutarch the apparition calls itself 'thy evil spirit, Brutus' and so it does in Shakespeare's dialogue; only from the stage direction do we learn that it is supposed to be the ghost of Caesar. Brutus makes no reference to it until he mentions his second meeting with the ghost just before his suicide. Its appearance in this scene is a return to the supernatural element that overshadowed the beginning of the play. Caesar himself is now an omen.

That you have wrong'd me The characters in this play waste no time in getting down to business; cf. I,1 and 2; III,1 and 2; IV,1.

noted Singled out for disgrace.

wherein i.e. in the course of the hearing.

Because I knew the man Cassius's shrewd judgement of individuals again confronts the idealism of Brutus, which allows for no exceptions.

nice Petty.

honours this corruption Provides an honourable excuse for those who are corrupt.

supporting robbers This is based on an isolated reference in Plutarch: 'Brutus . . . reminded him of the ides of March, the day when they had killed Caesar, who was not the scourge of mankind, but only abetted with his power those that were so.'

the mighty space . . . honours Brutus and Cassius were governors by previous appointment, each of a large province in the wealthy east, but this extravagant phrase is intended to belittle money transactions.

bait not me Don't worry me (like a dog).

older in practice . . . conditions Not clear, and misunderstood by Brutus in line 51. Apparently Cassius claims that longer experience in the army makes a better administrator. In ancient Rome there was rotation between army commands and political office.

Have mind upon your health As you value your life.

of noble men From men of character (i.e. unlike yourself).

elder The word was 'older'; 'elder' refers strictly to age. Cassius claimed longer experience.

For your life i.e. because you would have risked your life.

done that you should be sorry for i.e. condoned bribery.

honesty Here almost synonymous with 'honour' (cf. III,1,136).

idle i.e. blowing nothing before it.

respect Heed.

drop my blood for drachmas Let it fall in (metal) drops to be coined into drachmas.

indirection Malpractice, crooked methods.

rascal counters Mischievous pieces of money (strictly imitations for use in counting). Brutus despises the very thing he needs.

alone on Cassius On Cassius alone (and not on Brutus).

brav'd Defied.

Pluto's mine The mine identifies Pluto, god of the underworld (rather than a suggested emendation, Plutus, god of riches).

humour i.e. simply a state of mind.

yoked with a lamb i.e. instead of a strong-willed ox.

who, much enforced i.e. 'the flint' which, when struck with force.

hasty spark Cf. 'show of fire', I,2,174–5.

more years This makes the dispute in lines 31–4 seem childish now.

cynic Philosopher.

Know his humour . . . time i.e. accept his peculiarity on a more convenient occasion.

jigging Rhyming.

with her death . . . came i.e. news of her death and of the Caesarian preparations reached Brutus together.

swallow'd fire i.e. committed suicide, This was, according to Plutarch, a last resort when her friends kept weapons from her.

call in question Examine.

bending their expedition toward Leading their forces in the direction of.

proscription Condemnation to death in a published list.

farewell, Portia This (apparently prepared) display of his stoicism to a larger circle is unworthy of the wife in II,1. It has been suggested that one passage was inserted in place of the other, but both came to be printed.

art i.e. philosophy in theory, as distinct from putting it into practice. Cassius was an Epicurean, Brutus a Stoic.

marching to Philippi From Sardis in Asia Minor across the sea to Philippi in Macedonia, northern Greece, took them from spring to November, 42 BC. The swift action of the play, however, carries the spectator by a natural transition to the plains of Philippi in Act V.

I do not think it good Cassius is now seeking to thwart Brutus.

waste his means i.e. run out of supplies.

Omitted Neglected.

bound in shallows and in miseries i.e. restricted to shallow water (at the ebb), a miserable place for a ship to find itself in.

niggard with a little rest Grudge her (nature or necessity?) a niggardly hour or so.

knave Boy.

watch your pleasure Await your commands.

otherwise i.e. than sending a message to Cassius.

the pocket of my gown Anachronism, but in any age the place where an object is often found after much searching and blame having being cast on others!

mace A 'murderous' weapon, used in an arrest; 'leaden' suggests the heaviness of sleep; cf. 'honey-heavy dew of slumber' II,1,230.

That plays thee music i.e. who plays to bring on sleep.

leaf The Romans used rolls, not books.

How ill this taper burns! Ghostly influence.

stare Stand erect.

Thy evil spirit It is curious that having turned the mysterious phantom of history into the ghost of Caesar, Shakespeare, who wrote long speeches for the ghost of Hamlet's father, should have given it no more to say than Plutarch gives! However, taciturn as the ghost is, it intensifies the sense of impending tragedy and electrifies the audience with its few sepulchral syllables.

I shall see thee The same casual air with which he greeted news of Portia's death.

set on his powers betimes before March his army off early before mine. Brutus is always impatient of delays. And Shakespeare has here telescoped months of historic events into a few days.

Revision questions on Act IV

1 What part in the Triumvirate does Antony intend Lepidus to play?

2 What two reasons restrain Brutus from raising money by corrupt methods?

3 In how many ways does Brutus anger Cassius?

4 Who do you think is more to blame in the quarrel scene?

Act V

This Act is best summarized as a whole, as its five scenes are all successive stages in the one decisive conflict between the Caesarians and the Republicans. Like many of the Acts in the Folio edition of Shakespeare's plays it was printed without the numbering of scenes: that was done later by Nicholas Rowe and others. No stage could be barer or less in need of division into numbered scenes than this gloomy Act, filled with hostile challenges, farewell speeches and funeral orations. There are only two stage properties, a 'hill' to look out from and a rock to sit despondently on; the chief staging problem is the removal of dead bodies. Action is brief: swords are brandished or clash in skirmishes or are held out to be run upon; alarums are sounded, drums are beaten and trumpets blown; cries are heard in the distance, while close at hand famous names are shouted like slogans. In the dim light of evening and utter defeat there is the stillness of no hope, with whispered requests made in desperation and rejected in sorrow. Fate overtakes Brutus as he kills the killer of his erstwhile friend and patron, Julius Caesar.

The act opens on the plains of Philippi as the two armies approach each other. Contrary to Antony's judgement of what a sensible enemy would do, the Republicans have descended from the strategically stronger position in the hills, no doubt urged on by the impetuous Brutus, ever anxious for a result. Antony derides this move as a vain display of drummed-up courage. In a brief exchange Octavius shows his independence of the *older* man by insisting on leading the right wing. The stage direction 'March' suffices to indicate what would be a complicated manoeuvre for any one legion, let alone several! The leaders of the two sides confront each other across the stage, some attempt at negotiation being desirable before Roman fights Roman. The parley consists merely of a battle of wits, terminated by Octavius who draws his sword, determined to slay or be slain. He and Antony then rejoin their troops.

Cassius confesses to Messala that he has abandoned his Epicurean disregard of superstitions since birds of ill omen have replaced the eagles that had been frequenting his standards. He asks Brutus what he will do if they are defeated and is told by his friend that he will not dishonour himself in such a case, whether by being led captive in a triumph or committing suicide. Uncertain about ever meeting again, they exchange farewells (Scene 1).

Trumpets are heard, followed by the noise of fighting, as Brutus makes a brief appearance, to send Messala to some other legions (one legion averaged 5000 men), ordering them to take advantage of what seems irresolution among Octavius's men and advance to the attack. As Messala is Cassius's officer and supposedly acting in liaison with Brutus, this instruction might seem intended for Cassius's wing, but it must be Brutus throwing his men all at once into the battle (Scene 2).

We next see Cassius alone after endeavouring to stem the retreat of his men before Antony's forces, using the eagle of a runaway standard-bearer. Titinius meets him with the news that

Brutus's victorious troops are pillaging the tents of Octavius instead of rallying to the assistance of Cassius, whose tents in turn are being sacked and burnt by Antony's men. Seeing some cavalry at a distance, Cassius sends Titinius to find out whether they are friends or foes. Watching his progress from a nearby hill the slave Pindarus (his master having poor eyesight) reports what appears to be the seizure of Cassius's best friend, whereupon Cassius orders the slave to hold his sword (the one with which he helped to kill Caesar) while he runs on to it. Titinius enters, not a prisoner, but wearing one of Brutus's laurels of victory, and is stunned to see the dead body of his leader. While Messala sets off to find Brutus, Titinius, unassisted, takes his own life with the same sword. Brutus arrives and sees the influence of Caesar's spirit in the spectacle of two of the dictator's enemies self-slaughtered. Paying an emotional tribute to his dead colleague, Brutus prepares for the final onset (Scene 3).

The fighting comes closer and names are used as battle-cries, first 'Cato', by his son, and then 'Brutus' by his friend Lucilius, who, when called upon to surrender, identifies himself as Brutus, to allow the latter more chance of escaping. Remembering how Titinius died for Cassius' sake in the first battle, he invites the enemy soldier in this impersonation of Brutus to kill him. However, when Antony arrives he immediately realizes the deception and, after Lucilius utters a curious boast that Brutus will not be taken alive, orders him, as an equally valuable capture, to be kept in safe custody and treated well (Scene 4).

Accompanied by three remaining friends and a slave attendant, Brutus has withdrawn from the battle to a sheltered corner, where he promptly approaches each of the three friends in turn, none of whom have we met before, with a request to assist him in killing himself rather than that he should be taken prisoner. None of them assents; Volumnius, an old school friend, has just refused to perform this task when the approach of the enemy hastens matters, but not before Brutus has made his last oration, claiming future glory from the present defeat. Left alone with his slave, he persuades Strato to do what was 'not an office for a friend'. A last touch of the 'gentle Brutus' is seen in his words, 'Turn away thy face'. Octavius and Antony, accompanied by Lucilius and Messala, encounter Strato, who shows them Brutus on the ground, 'undefeated' by his foes. Octavius offers the followers of Brutus, including Strato, places in his service. It only remains for Antony's eloquence to pay a last tribute to the *one* 'honourable' man among the murderers of Caesar. Then Octavius makes the necessary arrangements for his burial (Scene 5).

Commentary

The substance of *Julius Caesar* is a network of personal relationships – strong affection, keen rivalry, intense loyalty, sharp suspicion, secret envy – and it reaches its highest development in the crisis and excitement of battle. We are shown the incipient jealousy of the two who emerge victors, the sad parting of two old comrades, the appearance of fresh faces and the discovery of other friendships. Also unshrinking sacrifice and final tributes, not overlooking the sturdy assistance of two devoted slaves in the despatch of their masters (a comment on 'freedom' in contemporary Rome that might well pass unnoticed).

Shakespeare has given himself a freer hand in these closing stages than anywhere else in the play. The whole campaign, covering eighteen months and great distances, even for the highly trained soldiery, is skilfully condensed into what seems hours. His chief alterations are personal: instead of Octavius being sick in his tent and Antony being caught by surprise, the four leaders are brought together face to face in a slanging match which blends past deeds with future prospects and creates the impression of a life and death contest between irreconcilables. The casualties at the real battle were heavy, even by the scale of modern warfare; tragedy here takes the form of three suicides.

Act V Scene 1

warn us Challenge us to fight.
I am in their bosoms i.e. I can read their innermost thoughts.
To visit other places To show their strength elsewhere.
and come down But they descend on us.
fearful bravery Formidable array. 'Brutus's army was inferior to Octavius Caesar's, in number of men; but for bravery and rich furniture, Brutus's army far excelled Caesar's' (Plutarch).
bloody sign 'The scarlet robe, which was the signal for battle, was hung out in the tents of Brutus and Cassius' (Plutarch).

even field The plain, as distinct from the hills.

I do not cross you; but I will do so This is the only hint Shakespeare lets fall of the division between Octavius and Antony, of which he had read so much and which he was to incorporate into *Antony and Cleopatra*.

shall we give sign of battle? Next moment the winner of the argument defers to his colleague.

on their charge When they attack.

Stir not Instruction to the troops behind him.

Words before blows Is Brutus commending the principle that talks should come before battle is joined, or sneering at his enemies for preferring to talk? The use of 'countrymen' highlights this civil war.

as you do Alluding to Brutus's reputation as an orator.

Hybla A mountain in Sicily, covered with fragrant flowers, making the local honey famous.

honeyless . . . stingless . . . soundless Cassius begins this exchange of verbal wit by saying that Antony's words are bitter enough to destroy all the honey of Hybla; Antony replies with what must be a question, 'Not stingless, too? (see line 38 below); Brutus retorts that if Antony has taken their stings, he has also acquired the bees' habit of buzzing first (an opening on which Antony pounces).

You show'd . . . neck Again Antony's imagination or a detailed account from an eye-witness supplies what he did not see himself.

flatterers i.e. of Caesar before stabbing him.

the cause The case at issue.

redder drops i.e. redder than drops of sweat.

Look This shortest of lines emphasizes the pause as he draws his sword.

three and thirty wounds Misprint for 'twenty-three'.

Caesar Brutus uses the name Octavius had adopted after his great-uncle's murder.

So I hope i.e. not to die.

on Brutus's sword i.e. by the hand of a traitor.

strain Race (the family of Julius).

masker One who takes part in masquerades (typical of the Elizabethan period).

stomachs Courage.

Why now, blow wind . . . bark A desperate state of mind, explained in his remarks to Messala. Cf. *Macbeth*, 'Blow wind! come, wrack!' (V,5,51).

on the hazard At stake.

as Pompey was He was defeated by Caesar at the battle of Pharsalia, 48 BC.

Epicurus A Greek philosopher (341-270 BC). The Epicurean ideal was the pleasure of the mind at rest, the Stoic ideal was virtue based on reason and not on emotion. The one degenerated into self-indulgence, hence 'epicurean', the other became synonymous with heroic endurance. Both schools based human judgement on the physical senses, thus ruling out the supernatural.

credit . . . presage Believe in omens.

former Foremost.

two mighty eagles A good omen.

ravens Birds of ill omen. Cf. *Macbeth*, 'The raven himself is hoarse' (I,5,39). The crows would be carrion-crows; kites ate offal.

A canopy most fatal i.e. their dark forms overhead, like a canopy above the bed of a sick man, foreshadow death.

Even so Brutus has finished his conversation with Lucilius and agrees with something the latter has just said.

The gods to-day stand friendly An optimistic greeting, in spite of the omens he has just mentioned, to balance the pessimistic suggestion he is about to make.

reason with Arrange for.

prevent The time of life Anticipate death.

He bears too great a mind Spoken with something of Caesar's Olympian grandeur. He does not explain how he can escape being a prisoner at a triumph, except by suicide.

this same day . . . begun A fatalistic mood given expression in an 'everlasting farewell'.

we'll smile indeed. We are reminded of the grim Cassius trying to hide his conspiratorial countenance in II,1.

O that a man . . . come Cf. his similar state of suspense before the assassination (II,1,63).

Act V Scene 2

Brutus's impatience brings disaster.
    This is one of the shortest scenes in Shakespeare.

bills Written instructions.
cold demeanour Lack of keenness.

Act V Scene 3

A swift change from Brutus's impetuous charge to Cassius's imminent defeat. There is not room at the end of the play for more than a very telescoped presentation of the battle. So foreshortened is it that there is some confusion; apart from the change of commands we are not told that Messala has been transferred by Cassius to Brutus, 'with the best of his legions' (Plutarch). These matters, however, are of less importance than the exhibition of moods and temperaments of the main characters.

Cassius's end is as tragic as Brutus's is to be. He who has seldom been fooled kills himself as a result of a misunderstanding of what he sees, though it is through the eyes of another. His birthday has the same fatal obsession for him that the ghost has for Brutus. The manner of his death confirms Brutus's belief that the spirit of Caesar is avenging itself on the conspirators. The dead dictator would indeed have found the battle an untidy mess, lacking generalship and proper communications: Brutus thought both wings had won, Cassius that both wings had lost.

ensign Standard-bearer, now lying nearby.
gave the word too early . . . fell to spoil Two tactical errors by Brutus told in three lines.
in your tents i.e. his men are pillaging and burning the tents in Cassius' rear.
This day i.e. his birthday (V,1,72).
his compass Its predetermined course.
on the spur At full speed.
Parthia In Asia Minor, where Cassius once did much to retrieve a heavy Roman defeat.
swore thee Made thee take an oath.
search Penetrate.
but change A victory for a defeat.
O my heart Cassius has just referred to Titinius as his best friend. The repetition of 'red' and 'setting' is highly emotional.
to night i.e. to bring on night.
O hateful Error This essay by Messala in poetic diction, with its artificial personifications and apostrophes, strikes a false note and it is doubtful as to whether it is Shakespeare's composition.
apt thoughts Minds too easily impressed.
Thasos An island in the Aegean Sea, off the coast a few miles away, mentioned by Plutarch.
discomfort us Discourage our troops.
ere night i.e. a second battle on the same day, beginning after 3 p.m. Shakespeare has strained tactics and logistics to the utmost.

Act V Scene 4

A snatch of fighting is inserted between the desperate suicides of Cassius and Brutus. It relieves the gloom somewhat and gives an opportunity for Lucilius to show *his* devotion to Brutus.

And I am Brutus ... Brutus These two lines (no indication of the speaker in the Folio) must be given to Lucilius, in keeping with what follows and to allow Brutus, after uttering the first line, to distance himself from his double.

Act V Scene 5

The audience is kept in suspense wondering whether Brutus will be taken alive or escape the disgrace. Death brings honour to him, as it brings final triumph to Caesar, whether the spirit of the dead dictator or his youthful heir. It also heals all wounds: the Antony who displayed the 'most unkindest cut of all' (III, 2) to a weeping crowd, who reminded Brutus of the hole he made in Caesar's heart, and who sneered at Brutus's honour and mocked his reasons, now acclaims him the 'noblest Roman of them all.'

The last words are spoken by the new Caesar, future master of the Roman world.

poor remains of friends Indicating complete defeat.
the torch-light This signal suggests the oncoming darkness. Statilius had been sent, through the enemy lines, to get information.
the pit The grave.
smatch Smack.
my master's man But Messala originated with Cassius.
entertain Accept into my service.
in a general . . . all Thinking honestly and without private malice of the common good.
call the field to rest Stop the fighting.

Revision questions on Act V

1 How many points of dramatic importance can you find in Scene 1?
2 Compare and contrast the deaths of Brutus and Cassius.
3 Write notes on the minor characters in this act, bringing out clearly their main traits.

Shakespeare's art in *Julius Caesar*
Setting and theme

Setting

Shakespeare had not at his elbow the accumulation of material on daily life in ancient Rome that has been acquired in centuries of research since his day. There were no handbooks with ample photographic illustrations and diagrams with which to recreate its urban civilization: temples and forums, colonnades and fountains; great wealth through the exploitation of vast provinces; highly organised and expensively equipped armies marching and counter-marching across continents; and huge mobs with little regular employment, but lavish free entertainment in vast arenas.

From the reading of classical literature, however, an interest had been aroused in ancient history, Greek myths, Roman legends and pagan philosophy, which last included Epicureanism with its emphasis on happiness and avoidance of pain, and Stoicism with its emphasis on reason and avoidance of emotion. Republican Rome had come to symbolize the authority of written law, the importance of an ordered society and the traditional rights of individual citizens (provided they were 'citizens'). With the breakdown, through personal rivalries, of proper government, there came into being the conception of an autocratic emperor in the person of Octavius, heir of Julius Caesar; the latter had been the first to regard himself as a permanent 'imperator' (instead of the hated 'rex'). Hence, after centuries of election and dynastic succession, Caesar was the equivalent of the Holy Roman Emperor of Shakespeare's day. The teaching of Latin in English schools and of some Greek in the upper forms created a consciousness of the Roman world as the fountain of civilization, and of its literature and arts as models for others to copy.

Shakespeare's audiences, therefore, knew something of the historical facts, but little of actual physical appearances: they saw nothing incongruous in those who acted as Romans wearing hose and doublet. Other details, today called 'anachronisms' because they did not belong to the 'period', would pass unnoticed. Today Caesar appears on the stage in a robe called a 'toga' (unless the play is being performed in modern dress), but embedded in the text of the play are a number of discrepancies, which we 'note' but do not condemn. This was Shakespeare's first venture into the classical era after dealing with a succession of English reigns; among other reasons for the change may be the publication a few years earlier of Plutarch's *Lives*. The following discrepancies are 'for the record' only.

It is Casca who, thanks to North's Plutarch, describes Caesar plucking open his 'doublet' before the crowd; as this incident takes place offstage we need not bother to wonder whether it had been put on under the purple robe Caesar is reported to have worn at the festival. Next day, however, when his Elizabethan impersonator donned the robe for the Senate meeting (II,2,107), he must have dispensed with the doublet or it would have had to be stripped rapidly from his body in the brief interval between assassination and funeral. Otherwise a doublet on the corpse would obscure the gaping wounds – as would another discrepancy, the 'coffin' (III,2,108) in place of a Roman bier. Shakespeare had pictured a Tudor funeral halted in the middle of a Roman marketplace.

The conspirators do not draw their togas over their heads, but pull their 'hats' about their ears and bury their faces in their cloaks. The sick Logarius wears a 'kerchief'. When at home Brutus reads in a 'study', a room no archaeologist has yet unearthed on a Roman site. Strictly speaking, a 'taper' (II,1,35) was used to light a candle fixed in a candelabra. The Romans had more sophisticated illumination than generally understood, but they still, like the Elizabethans, had recourse to steel upon flint (line 36) for the vital 'spark' (IV,3,110-11).

Cassius bids Cinna attach (with wax) one of his bills to the statue of Brutus's reputed ancestor, an Elizabethan practice (with printed ones), but not seen in ancient Rome. Instead of unrolling his manuscript volume Brutus finds the 'leaf' he has turned down, as if it were a printed book, of pocket size for use during a campaign, small enough to have been thrust into his Elizabethan 'pocket' and forgotten when he came to look for it. When Cassius accuses Brutus of listing his 'faults' he thinks of him as scribbling in a 'notebook'; in 44 BC the latter would have been incising his memoranda on small waxed tablets. Shakespeare's Lucius probably played the Tudor lute rather than a classical lyre.

Theme

Shakespeare's idea of good government was probably a bene-
volent autocracy. Rulers might have their weaknesses, but
violent revolt against the established order generally brought
untold suffering and defeated its own ends.

Brutus sought to restore freedom to a people incapable of
preserving law and order without a strong ruler. Idealism, too, is
admirable in itself, but any important enterprise, whether
honourable or dishonourable, requires shrewd dealing, as that
English queen knew who was just drawing to the close of a very
astute reign.

Contemporary politics may provide interesting parallels (such
as the question of Elizabeth's successor, the plots against her life
and the behaviour of the London populace), but they have
probably little or nothing to do with the construction of the play.
Shakespeare was more interested in the dramatic presentation
of a famous assassination and in the motives and blunders of the
conspirators. This piece of treacherous mass stabbing had to be
enacted on the stage in full view of the audience, simply because
it was familiar to them from their own reading. As if to avoid an
anticlimax after the horror of this deed, the playwright made of
Brutus a character of more enduring interest than his historical
counterpart: an idealist torn between personal loyalty and philo-
sophical principle, who strikes a foul blow in what is for him a
noble cause and yet persists in honourable gestures that bring
disaster on him and his associates.

Honour surrounds Brutus like an aura, and this might seem
to be the theme of the play. A lofty moral outlook with a bookish
background, divorced from practical common sense in dealing
with others, leads to tragic failure, as do ambition, jealousy and
other human weaknesses in Shakespeare's greatest plays. An
exaggerated sense of honour is a dangerous defect in a conspirator, especially a leader in a conspiracy. There are variations
on this theme worth noticing.

Taking his cue from Brutus, Cassius declares honour to be the
'subject' of his interview with him; later, after having enlarged to
his friend on the dishonourable kind of existence led in the
shadow of such a man as Caesar, he remarks to himself how
easily Brutus's honourable metal may be twisted out of shape.
He introduced Casca to an enterprise that has become to him
one of 'honourable–dangerous consequence'. After listening

(off-stage) to Brutus's speech, Antony also uses this declared 'honour' of Brutus with skilful irony, each repetition increasing in severity, until he brands the whole group as 'traitors'.

In the last encounter the death of Brutus is tinged with supreme honour; at first, to die on his sword would confer honour on the victim; then it is vital to his friends that no enemy should gain honour by slaying Brutus or capturing him alive; finally, the slave who holds the sword is known to his master as having an honourable record!

In an age of conflicting loyalties (in which this play of conflicting loyalties was written), the question of personal honour would be of absorbing interest to all immersed in the often treacherous politics of Tudor England.

The characters

Julius Caesar

Always I am Caesar

The greatest man of ancient times appears in the play chiefly as an affected autocrat, pretending to a courage and determination he obviously does not possess, superstitious to a degree, and surrounded by obsequious flatterers.

Shakespeare's knowledge of Roman history, derived as it is mainly from Plutarch, was bound to be faulty, but he seems deliberately to have selected the weak points in Caesar's character and omitted any reference to the far-reaching schemes of improvement planned by Caesar. When Shakespeare's Brutus sends Lucius to consult the calendar, no thought crosses his mind that the reformer of that calendar was none other than the great Julius.

There are dramatic reasons for this depreciation of the soldier-statesman: (1) an audience filled with admiration would have been revolted by his killing, especially when it took place on the stage; (2) Brutus would have paled in comparison, and his death would have been less a tragedy than the successful end of a punitive expedition.

Stress had to be laid on Caesar's ambition to be king. He must seem less a great man, more a threat to the liberties of Rome. His will, then, is absolute; the people show their disapproval, but a servile senate is about to gratify him with a crown to be worn outside Italy. Opposition has to be secret and furtive.

Caesar is made to behave as if he were already king. He executes the tribunes for insulting his statues; he issues peremptory commands, listened to in silence and obeyed instantly; he frequently refers to himself in the third person. On the fatal day, the scene at the Capitol takes on the aspect of a court, even before the royal title has been bestowed by the 'graybeards' hovering in the background. Only recently made aware, by Decius Brutus, of the intended honour, and sublimely unaware of what is really intended by the petitioners crouching at his feet, he makes a show of royal authority:

Caesar   Are we all ready? What is now amiss
             That Caesar and his senate must redress?
Metellus   Most high, most mighty, and most puissant Caesar (III, 1,31–3)

If the conspirators lacked any spur to raise their hidden daggers (and in *Plutarch* the magnitude of the deed awes them and makes their first strokes ineffective), it is supplied in the words of the occupant of the golden chair: 'I spurn thee like a cur out of my way' (III, 1,46), and 'I could be well moved, if I were as you'.

It is no wonder that Cassius describes him as a god before whose nod others must bow, but Casca reports him in a different light when face to face with the citizens. While Caesar sees no harm in telling the Senate the truth – that he simply is not coming – on the other hand, he acts a part before the crowd: he dissimulates his desire for the crown, yet is so cut to the heart by their too enthusiastic applause of his refusal of it, that in a fit he offers them his throat, afterwards apologizing humbly for his strange behaviour.

Physical defects like this seem to justify the otherwise envious speech of Cassius. Casca's account of the epileptic attack reminds us of the same 'fever' whose progress Cassius watched in Spain. The deafness in the left ear which Shakespeare added, he added as an ironic continuation of 'always I am Caesar'.

Other weaknesses are rendered all the more damning (and, incidentally, all the more noticeable) by clumsy attempts to disguise them: 'I rather tell thee what is to be fear'd/Than what I fear; for always I am Caesar.' He wished to be thought more dangerous than danger itself. It is impossible he should make a mistake: 'Know, Caesar doth not wrong.' At home his mind is made up for him, first by Calphurnia and then by Decius, yet he would seem inflexible:

But I am constant as the northern star,
Of whose true-fix'd and resting quality
There is no fellow in the firmament. (III, 1,60–2)

His first words on each of his appearances are concerned with superstition: the fertility rites of the Lupercalia, sacrificing for omens, and the Soothsayer's warning. In spite of brave words: 'It seems to me most strange that men should fear' – he is much disturbed by Calphurnia's dream and is relieved to have Decius's interpretation of it.

Nevertheless, something finer in the man is discerned in little glimpses, such as the reason for his rejection of Artemidorus's petition: 'What touches us ourself shall be last serv'd', and the good-natured banter with which he greets his callers. Brutus finds 'no personal cause to spurn at him', though he is perhaps willing to overlook faults in a benefactor.

Caesar, unlike Brutus, possesses some insight into others' characters. Of Cassius he says. 'He is a great observer', and, though he openly dismisses the Soothsayer as a 'dreamer', his secret thoughts are full of the prophecy.

His true greatness, however, is revealed only after his death. In striking him down, Brutus aims at his spirit, but, though he slays the body, he cannot destroy that spirit which survives not only in his heirs, but in the more terrible world of the supernatural. Caesar is, indeed, mightier in death than in life. It is as if the manner of his death raises him above all criticism. When he exclaims, 'Hence! wilt thou lift up Olympus?' we still smile at his affectation of greatness; but in a short space we are sobered by the magnitude of the fall.

Antony addresses his body as if it can still hear:

O, pardon me, thou bleeding piece of earth,
That I am meek and gentle with these butchers!
Thou art the ruins of the noblest man
That ever lived in the tide of times. (III, 1,254–7)

He uses Caesar's mantle to recall his brilliant victories as well as to stigmatize his murderers individually; he uncovers Caesar's wounds to arouse the pity once felt by Caesar for others; he reads his will to prove he was more generous than ambitious.

Caesar's funeral unleashes the violence of the mob: 'Most noble Caesar, we'll revenge his death.' His ghost is an avenging spirit striking despair into the heart of the least guilty of his slayers: 'O Julius Caesar, thou art mighty yet!' Brutus and Cassius die with his name on their lips.

Brutus

This was the noblest Roman of them all

Shakespeare's Caesar covets a kingly crown; his Brutus sets honour above all merely material ambitions. In this man lives – and dies – the last spark of that ancient republican virtue which put public interest before personal advancement, which preserved a sense of dignity and responsibility in the conduct of affairs. which set its face against corruption and luxurious living, and which allowed personal dictatorship only in time of emergency. It is this traditional virtue which, while it leads him to help in assassinating the man who threatens the liberties of the State and then to make decisions which prove fatal to the enterprise, yet commands the respect of his fellows, of the people at large and, in the end, of his enemies. There is no man but honours 'the noble Brutus', but the freedom for which he gives his life is extinct in a generation that must have a Caesar.

Brutus values his honour more than his own safety:

Set honour in one eye and death i' the other,
And I will look on both indifferently;
For let the gods so speed me as I love
The name of honour more than I fear death. (I, 2,85–8)

He puts the conspirators on their honour:

What need we any spur but our own cause
To prick us to redress? (II, 1,123–4)

He spares Antony, so that their action may seem more honourable, 'We shall be call'd purgers, not murderers.' He bases his claim to a hearing on his reputation: 'Believe me for mine honour, and have respect to mine honour, that you may believe.'

Sooner than the dishonour of going 'bound to Rome', he falls on his sword, held by a man whose life has had 'some smatch of honour in it'. Not even defeat can stain 'the even virtue of our enterprise', for, in his own eyes, he falls not as a traitor, but as a martyr in the cause of freedom. As Antony says of him (V,5,68), 'This was the noblest Roman of them all.'

This sense of honour, typical of a philosopher and reputed descendant of the Brutus of the early republic, has two aspects: (1) a virtuous life, (2) loyalty to Republican traditions or 'freedom'.

Brutus is outstanding among the characters of the play for his transparent honesty, self-restraint and fortitude. His honesty makes him widely respected: 'O, he sits high in all the people's hearts.' His calmness rarely deserts him: when Popilius Lena speaks to Caesar, Brutus steadies Cassius with a word; when the ghost materializes, he is almost flippant. His Stoicism wrings admiration from his friends: 'Even so great men great losses should endure.'

Brutus loves Caesar, but he loves Rome more, and to him the soul of Rome is that ancient liberty handed down from the days when his ancestor expelled the last of the kings. He cannot see that the liberty has degenerated into licence (represented in the play by popular admiration for favourite generals who pamper the citizens with shows), nor is he capable of foreseeing that, by removing one beneficent despot, he will bring about a worse tyranny. To him the rule of one man reduces the rest to slaves: 'Who is here so base that would be a bondman?' The spectacle of Caesar's quasi-royal power offends him, not because the dictator is an ordinary man (which so enrages Cassius), but because everyone seems to be at his beck and call:

Brutus had rather be a villager
Than to repute himself a son of Rome
Under these hard conditions as this time
Is like to lay upon us. (I, 2,170–3)

If Caesar is invested with such authority for life, sheer despotism may result:

Th'abuse of greatness is, when it disjoins
Remorse from power. (II, 1,18–19)

There is in Brutus a touch of personal pride in his reputation for honesty and philosophy. He is 'arm'd so strong in honesty' that he neither fears Cassius's threats nor spares his faults; he 'bears too great a mind' to be taken alive; he even stoops to pretence over the loss of his wife, when, hearing the news for the *second* time, he utters the laconic remark, 'Why, farewell, Portia'.

His scrupulous honesty finds *reasons* to justify every action. Unfortunately these reasons are usually too abstract and un-suited to the circumstances of very real problems. He argues to himself in proverbs: 'It is the bright day that brings forth the adder.'

Caesar has not yet proved himself a tyrant, but he may do so if crowned, so the serpent must be killed in the shell. Or he brings sentiment into the matter. There must be no mangling of Caesar's 'limbs' and, since Caesarism cannot be destroyed with-out shedding the blood of Caesar, 'Let's carve him as a dish fit for the gods.'

In discussions concerning the omission of an oath, the 'sound-ing' of Cicero, the question of Antony's fate, permission for Antony to address the crowd, and the march to Philippi, he overbears Cassius with a flood of eloquence based on such abstract reasons as the word of a Roman or the sacred character of their enterprise.

He is so blinded by worship of reason that:

1 He expects it to explain away all opposition – 'Our reasons are so full of good regard/That were you, Antony, *the son of Caesar*,/You should be satisfied.'
2 He believes the citizens will be convinced by logical arguments – 'public reasons shall be rendered/Of Caesar's death'.
3 He expects others to yield to him – 'Good reasons must, of force, give place to better.'
4 And therefore he is not easily impressed by the reasoning of others. He seems to lend a more attentive ear to the distant acclamations than to Cassius's long tirade against Caesar; only when his wife reveals her wound is he impressed enough to share his secret with her.

Antony seizes on Brutus's devotion to honour and his fetish of reason when, at the funeral, he treats the one with irony and the other with sarcasm: 'they are wise and honourable/And will, no doubt, with reasons answer you.'

Taking men at their word, he is too honest to suspect ulterior motives. He trusts Antony to keep his promise not to cast any blame; the applause of the crowd serves only to increase his confidence. All through he fails to see that Cassius is 'humouring' him – using him as a tool for his own ends.

At the very end, Brutus sees the avenging spirit of Caesar as responsible for his disaster, not his own misjudgements or any betrayal of his trust in others. This idealism is the offspring of philosophic study. Of Brutus the student we have one brief glimpse in his tent before the fatal battle: while others sleep, he reads on into the night, finding solace in some favourite philosopher. Assassination does not occur to him till he is prompted by Cassius and his 'bills'. The need of the moment seems to call him from more congenial pursuits into the fray of political action. Only Brutus could say:

So are we Caesar's friends, that have abridg'd
His time of fearing death. (III, 1,104–5)

It is as the high priest of Republican freedom, on whose altar ambition has been sacrificed, that he commands: 'Stoop, Romans, stoop,/And let us bathe our hands in Caesar's blood.' It is a crime which he, unlike Macbeth, could not have committed in his own interests. His nature ordinarily is full of gentleness and consideration for others. He thinks more of his wife's health than his own; he hastens to assure old Publius that he is quite safe; twice he refrains from waking the sleeping Lucius, and makes his messengers sleep on cushions in his tent. None but a slave can be persuaded to put Brutus's gentle soul out of its misery.

But the murder of Caesar is a crime, and all the more shocking as Brutus is Caesar's 'angel'. His victim dies with his name on his lips. This contradictory character of gentle murderer, partly explainable as the victory of patriotism over friendship, is also to be accounted for by minor contradictory elements in his nature. Soon after he mockingly bids the 'monstrous visage' of conspiracy to hide itself, he advises the very same conspiracy to 'look fresh and merrily'. After rating Cassius for corrupt methods of acquiring money, he upbraids him for not giving him some of it. Although he has scornfully pointed out that the mercurial Antony is too fond of life to 'take thought and die for Caesar', he coolly tells Antony's servant: 'Thy master is a wise and valiant Roman;/I never thought him worse.' Finally, he who blamed Cato for suicide runs on his own sword.

There is, too, a certain cold aloofness, an air of always being in the right, which exasperates Cassius in particular: 'Brutus, this sober form of yours hides wrongs.' Brutus feels throughout an antipathy to Cassius, or rather to Cassius's bad qualities. After the quarrel that arises out of merciless fault-finding, he forgives calmly where Cassius does impulsively, then proceeds to browbeat him once more with reasons.

In the same way he calmly condemns Caesar for what he *may* do, calmly kisses his hand in joint petition, and calmly stabs his mortally wounded benefactor. The assassination is not without effect upon that nobility which others admire to the end. He becomes superstitious: 'I know my hour is come.' He boasts of his honour: 'Young man, thou couldst not die more honourable'; and finally, with tears in his eyes, begs his friends to kill him.

These defects, however, pass almost unnoticed beside the generous farewell to Cassius and the pathos of his own last words: 'Caesar, now be still:/I kill'd not thee with half so good a will.' Antony pays him the finest tribute in the play in his last speech, and Octavius treats his remains 'according to his virtue', surrendering his tent for the night so that they may rest there, 'order'd honourably'.

Cassius

Such men are dangerous

Caius Cassius should have been the leader of the conspiracy. Instead, having organized it and, by his tactful prompting, won over Brutus to give it the character of an honourable enterprise, he resigns the leadership to his fellow praetor. The politician takes second place to the philosopher. Had he had his way with Antony, the story would have ended very differently.

The characters of the two men are in many respects complementary. Cassius lacks the idealism and self-control of Brutus, as Brutus lacks the shrewdness and fervour of Cassius. Just as each has more intimate friendships, Cassius with Titinus, Brutus with Lucilius, so their association is not a happy one. It is to the credit of the hasty Cassius that his forbearance keeps the partnership in being so long, but this self-effacement proves the undoing of them all. Brutus loses some of his nobility when he takes a hand in the other's undertaking, while Cassius, under the influence of a loftier mind, develops the better side of his nature. The man who detests the superiority of Caesar tacitly admits his inferiority to Brutus.

Yet the love of freedom in men like Cassius, though they are envious and 'be never at heart's ease/Whiles they behold a greater than themselves' may be more deep-seated and fervent than that of those who 'love words better' (V,1,28). Like Brutus, having taken his stand, Cassius is not lacking in personal courage.

In Cassius good and weak points are surprisingly blended. He is tactful in his approaches to Brutus and Casca, yet his temper easily gets the better of him. His hearing is acute, but his eyesight poor: quick to recognize Casca by his voice and Cinna by his gait (i.e. the sound of his footsteps), he is so unable to see at a distance that he trusts to another's eyes in a critical situation, with fatal results. His shrewd knowledge of men is seen when he appeals to the love of freedom in Brutus and to the love of office in Antony; yet he is blind to his own exaggerated sense of wrong; three times he accuses Brutus of wronging him. Beside the gentle Brutus he is harsh and unattractive, but at heart he has a more human, more affectionate, more loyal side (after all Caesar was not Cassius's friend). In response to Brutus's pledge, he cries: 'Fill, Lucius, till the wine o'erswell the cup;/I cannot drink too much of Brutus' love.'

Cassius is not the villain of the play (if there is one, it is Decius). His tendency is to brood over injustices until he is desperate and scorns the world around him. Rome has 'lost the breed of noble bloods' and, if Caesar is a 'wolf', Romans are 'sheep'. His shrewd, practical nature foresees the danger in Antony, and when he cannot have his own way and have him murdered too, he tries to pin him down to a definite statement of support or hostility, so that the conspirators may know how they stand with regard to him.

He has a much greater insight into character than Brutus; for instance, Casca's pose of 'bluntness' does not deceive him, and he has a much better idea than Brutus generally how to tackle people – friends and foes. He is not, however, far-seeing enough to realize that though Brutus would give prestige he would bungle the conspiracy. He condones bribery in time of emergency, but, sooner than live in awe of 'so vile a thing as Caesar', he will make it a point of honour to take his own life, which he frequently and in a rather theatrical manner threatens to do.

Envious, cruel, choleric, Cassius has the gift of making friends in greater measure than the calm, gentle, high-souled Brutus. Lucilius is gratified to find Brutus, as he forecast, the same noble self, honoured in death, but Titinus plunges Cassius's sword into his own heart, saying, 'Brutus, come apace,/And see how I regard Caius Cassius.'

Mark Antony

A shrewd contriver

The story of Antony is continued in *Antony and Cleopatra*, in which play the 'peevish schoolboy' crushes the 'masker and reveller'. In *Julius Caesar* little is seen or suggested of Antony's military genius, which made him Caesar's second in command, or his self-indulgence which eventually led to his downfall. His part in the play is that of a quick-witted schemer and powerful orator. There is an attractive dash and fire about him which makes him stand out against the calm Brutus and the crafty Cassius. His love of music, plays, and popular festivals (noted by Caesar) is a mask which deceives Brutus, but not Cassius: 'we shall find of him/A shrewd contriver.'

For his part, indeed, Antony seems to have been quite unsuspicious of foul play. He reassures Caesar, whose sharp eye has detected the look on Cassius's face: 'Fear him not, Caesar; he's not dangerous;/He is a noble Roman and well given.'

In the general confusion he escapes to Caesar's house, whence, having possessed himself of the dead man's papers, he ventures forth with the effrontery of the born gambler, staking all on his knowledge of Brutus. First he sends a messenger to Brutus as the new dictator, declaring that, given *reasons*, he will go over to his side. On the strength of Brutus's word of *honour*, he returns to the scene of the crime and faces the conspirators, an unarmed man amongst armed men, the one hampered by no moral scruples, the many hampered by the moral scruples of their leader.

He feels his way with them exactly as he does later with the crowd. He praises Caesar and he praises the conspirators; one moment he shakes hands with each of the murderers, the next turns aside to weep over the murdered; he speaks slightingly of himself:

My credit now stands on such slippery ground,
That one of two bad ways you must conceit me,
Either a coward or a flatterer. (IV, 1,191–3)

His request to be allowed to mourn Caesar in a public speech 'as becomes a friend' seems as guileless as his production of and refusal to read the will.

Left by himself, his pent-up fury breaks out in a hideous prophecy of civil war, even though the issue is still uncertain. There is no acting here. Antony is capable of a personal devotion as great as the devotion of Brutus to an idea. In the next scene he is at his best, ringing the changes on humility, accusation, reminiscence, indignation, pathos, defiance, modesty, rebuke, until he reaches his climax: 'Here was a Caesar! when comes such another?'

Left alone once more, he reveals even more clearly (cf. III,1,291–4) the cunning which has underlain the whole performance: 'Now let it work. Mischief, thou art afoot,/Take thou what course thou wilt!' He has of set purpose aroused the populace to fury, and their violent lust for revenge fills him with a fierce joy in the coming destruction: 'Fortune is merry,/And in this mood will give us everything.'

His cunning in flattering Brutus into giving him the fatal permission is as shameless as the cunning of Decius in flattering Caesar into making his fatal appearance at the Capitol.

The proscription scene portrays Antony at his worst – cruel, mercenary, cynical. He ticks off with zest the names of the victims, proceeds to tamper with the will and boasts of the way he exploits Lepidus. (A historical note may be of interest here: fleeing destitute from Octavius, Antony arrived in the camp of Lepidus, where his tongue won for him the soldiers' support, with the result that Lepidus was soon commander in name only.)

On the other hand, he can show quite sincere appreciation of others, for, in addition to the reference to Cassius quoted on p.78 he praises the self-sacrifice of Lucilius: 'I had rather have/ Such men my friends than enemies.' He gives orders that Brutus shall not be slain; and when Brutus lies before him, he utters a tribute that is among the finest in the language.

Portia

A woman well-reputed

Brutus is matched with a noble wife. Loving and practical, she seeks to share his anxiety as, on the other hand, Caesar's wife seeks to make him share hers. Calphurnia is without any distinctive trait, save that she knows her husband's weakness for disowning fear. She allows herself to be overridden, but Portia is determined to share the secret that comes between her and Brutus – out of a desire to help him, not out of idle curiosity – and tests her self-control to prove to him, when other arguments fail, that she can keep it. That she is so upset at Brutus's silence shows that usually Brutus found her worthy to share his secrets. Brutus treats Portia as a companion, whereas Caesar treats Calphurnia as a child to be put in her place. Portia's attempt to find out what is troubling Brutus is worthy of the daughter and wife of Stoics; in fact it is her pride that she is 'so fathered and so husbanded' that gives her added strength and determination.

Like Lady Macbeth, she is bold in her husband's interests and, like her, too, finds afterwards that she has 'a man's mind, but a woman's might'. Her constancy fails at the crisis (just as Lady Macbeth swoons) and nearly betrays the secret so well kept by others. For fear Lucius may have overheard her prayer for success, she pretends to be anxious about a petition and sends the boy on a frivolous errand. The success of her husband's enemies and the suspense of separation make her so desperate that she is deprived of all means of inflicting a really fatal wound on herself, but a woman of her determination cannot be foiled. Far away, her husband's grief is suppressed – an angry scene with Cassius, and then 'to our work alive'.

Octavius Caesar

I was not born to die on Brutus' sword

Caesar's heir is a man of few words. When Antony, on the score of being an older man, has his way with Lepidus he keeps his own counsel, trusting nobody (IV,1,50). It is when the critical battle is about to be joined that he asserts himself (V,1,20ff.). Impatient of 'words before blows', Octavius draws his sword, the sword of 'another Caesar', and finally cuts the argument short with a challenge to the field. His spirit of cold ruthlessness is a foil to Antony's burning vengeance; his final words leave with the audience an impression that the future lies with him.

Minor characters

Other conspirators. A number of embittered aristocrats, remnants of Pompey's party, seek to give their revolt the appearance of a popular movement for freedom. They are too well-known for what they are, so they borrow the name of Brutus but, though strengthened by his reputation for honesty, they are destroyed through his decisions. Casca, Decius, Cinna, Metellus, Trebonius, and Ligarius play individual parts up to the reentry of Antony, after which their fates are no longer of dramatic importance.

Casca is a creation of Shakespeare's (in Plutarch he is conspicuous merely for a rather ineffectual first blow). His character is almost chameleon-like in its changes. Appearing first prominent among the flatterers, he later retails the incident of the crown with a cynical indifference that cloaks a real understanding of the issue – 'to my thinking, he would fain have had it'. Cassius detects the 'wit' under the 'rudeness' and encounters him when all his latent superstition has been roused to a frenzy of fear by the storm. The revelation of a desperate enterprise brings out the bold conspirator. He will go as far as any one to ensure success: no 'fleering tell-tale' himself, he is anxious for the oath of secrecy to be sworn, and he gives the prearranged signal with fierce determination, 'Speak, hands, for me!' Such is his admiration for Brutus (I,3,157–60) that a word from the latter causes him to contradict himself (II,1,150–53).

Decius is the hypocritical flatterer. Having wound himself into the affections of Caesar he betrays him by rousing his fear of ridicule. He cunningly thrusts himself in front of Artemidorus, as if aware of the denial in that 'schedule' of the very love he has just professed. His real name was Decimus Brutus, Decius being an error by Amlot, the French translator of Plutarch.

Cinna must have had a rapid 'gait' to deliver all Cassius's papers in the time. His hated name results in the death of an innocent man.

Trebonius is a good conversationalist. Caesar has 'an hour's talk in store' for him, and his ready tongue draws Antony aside. Certain that the reveller will 'laugh at this hereafter', he is surprised to find Antony 'fled to his house amazed'.

Ligarius, rising from a sickbed, personifies the blind devotion inspired in others by Brutus. He plays no part in the assassination.

Cicero, though not one of the conspirators, shares their fate. His fiery eyes are the only hint of his fiery speeches against Antony. Shakespeare's reason for his omission is not the caution of an old statesman, but his characteristic determination to have his way. The orator would not relish being 'cross'd in conference' as Cassius is. His philosophic calmness in the storm is a foil to Casca's breathlessness.

Lepidus. If Cassius is to be condemned for turning his friendship with Brutus to his own advantage, what are we to say of Antony's treatment of Lepidus? In history by no means the cipher Shakespeare makes him appear, he merely serves here to illustrate further the more unpleasant side of Antony's character.

Caesar was unfortunate in that so large a conspiracy was not somehow given away. The gipsy-like *Soothsayer* does his best as mouthpiece of the supernatural, and his cryptic warning is followed by a night of terrifying manifestations, but it is the petition of *Artemidorus*, teacher of rhetoric to politicians – a more practical and documented notification of specific danger – that really increases the dramatic tension. In the street the two come together: to Caesar's jaunty greeting the prophet of woe merely makes a sinister rejoinder, whereas Artemidorus does attempt to save the great man's life, only to be out-manœuvred by Decius (is this wily conspirator aware of the 'dynamite' in the proffered paper?) and dismissed as a madman by a Caesar risen far above petty personal interests.

The Tribunes

These held an ancient office (originally two in number) which looked after the interests of the *plebs*, the common people. In the confused state of the first century BC they were often nominated instead of elected and were partisans of a particular party. Flavius is the senior and gives instructions; Marullus is youthful and passionate, his manner of speaking to the crowd anticipating that of Antony.

The Commoners or Plebeians

If Caesar is represented in a bad light, so are the common people. There are dramatic reasons for this, too. In Plutarch they respect Brutus but preserve a stony silence, while they howl down Cinna. So, though described as a 'multitide of rakehels of all sorts', they do not swerve from their allegiance to the champion of the popular party, Caesar. In Shakespeare they are as enthusiastic for Brutus at first as they are enraged against him afterwards.

Again, Pompey had actually left the people's cause for the senatorial party, whereas in the first Scene they appear to have easily transferred their affections from one favourite to another. Not only is this Scene a preparation for the greater fickleness to follow, but it provides two contrasting examples in the influence of suggestion on the mass mind. The tribunes *rebuke* them for their cruelty:

You blocks, you stones, you worse than senseless things!
O you hard hearts, you cruel men of Rome,
Knew you not Pompey? (I, 1,35–7)

And they vanish 'tongue-tied in their guiltiness'. Antony *arouses* them by denying their hard-heartedness:

You are not wood, you are not stones, but men;
And being men, hearing the will of Caesar,
It will inflame you, it will make you mad. (III, 2,144–6)

and they are mad with rage. Similarly with the workings of mass emotion. When made to reflect on the past glories of Pompey the whole crowd is sad and silent; when made to look on the mangled body of Caesar it is fierce and violent.

In the great funeral scene itself, the methods of the two orators are in strong contrast. Brutus, speaking in flexible, balanced prose, convinces them that, with Caesar out of the way, they are now all free men. He lectures them on the ambition of Caesar and offers them a place in the new commonwealth. Antony, in the more emotional medium of verse and employing the simplest expressions, seeks to bring home to them the greatness of their loss. He begins as the humblest of citizens who can only feel like them, knows no more than they do, loved Caesar as they did. He comes down from the pulpit and becomes one of them; he weeps and soon they weep; he mourns Caesar and soon they are all mourning Caesar; Caesar was Antony's friend – and Brutus's – and soon he appears their friend as well. In their sorrow and anger they forget the will, just as they forgot Caesar's refusal of the crown when Brutus said he was ambitious; when the great man's friendship takes the very tangible form of seventy-five drachmas, they forget all about the wonderful new commonwealth promised them by Brutus.

Their exclamations show their inability to hold more than one idea in their heads at once. Their unruliness shows their need of a strong man; they can think only in terms of that autocracy which in name they have rejected: 'Let him be Caesar.' Brutus's ideal of freedom is illusory; the people are unfitted for it. They depend on a spokesman or champion, even if it be only a cobbler bandying puns. All they are good at is shouting.

Their importance in the play is twofold: (1) as a chorus expressing feelings aroused by speakers, and a living background to the interplay of character that is the substance of the drama; (2) a visible force in deciding the fate of the conspirators, which is the counterpart of the invisible force of the supernatural.

One may suspect other than dramatic reasons for this portrayal of the crowd. The attitude of Casca (whose character is Shakespeare's invention) is that of the aristocracy (Roman or Elizabethan). There is more than a suspicion of the 'rabblement' who poured into the pit from the narrow streets across the Thames and clapped or hissed the actors on the stage. It was a lively mob that would line London streets, cheering some noble earl one day as a conquering hero, then hooting him as a traitor before the year was out.

The Officers

In the last two acts the lesser *dramatis personae* are almost completely changed. The body of conspirators is dispersed to meet their individual fates somewhere else; only their leaders are here. At the head of their respective armies they have, however, their staff officers to converse with. Antony and Octavius have no such escort on the stage, only a panting messenger: they have no need of more, as all they have to do is issue commands. With the other two it is different: they require close friends to whom they can unburden themselves. Cassius has two – *Messala*, to whom he confides his superstitious fears about his birthday, and the devoted *Titinius*, unexpectedly faithful unto death and rendering a tribute more moving than that of Brutus. His suicide reveals a Cassius to whom a follower can be as true as those of whom Brutus is to boast later on. Inspired by his example, *Lucilius* (who has described to Brutus all the signs of the cooling friendship of Cassius) does not wait for the death of his leader, but offers a bribe to the enemy soldiers to kill him in his impersonation of Brutus. He is instead taken as a valuable prize. Messala and he are induced to join the victors – that reconciliation among the survivors together with deep mourning for the dead which marks the end of a Shakespearian tragedy.

The Attendants

Of the two attendants who materialize at the eleventh hour to help their masters to die honourably, *Pindarus*, a slave from Parthia, flees in search of a world in which to enjoy freedom from Roman authority; *Strato*, an unknown quantity who has taken the place of Lucius (and inherited his practice of sleeping when not on duty), is credited by Brutus with sufficient honour to qualify him to hold the fatal sword (an impossible service for Lucius). His bold utterance makes such an impression on the future Caesar that he is taken into his service.

Of the boy *Lucius* we do not know whether he is bond or free, but his obvious affection for his master, whose 'gentle' nature finds expression in his treatment of him, probably enlists more sympathy on the part of the audience for Brutus than all his idealistic speeches. Though seemingly untouched by events around him, Lucius is not without intelligence, as when he is sent by Portia with a message to her husband. His yawns underline his master's studious nights and nocturnal visitors. Always ready to catch up on missing sleep, at Sardis he tries to do justice to 'Music and a Song', but his tired fingers are overcome by 'murderous slumber'. The broken melody of his lyre is soon to be replaced by the flourish of trumpets; meanwhile its 'sleepy tune' subdues the atmosphere of recent dissension and debate to a silence that is filled with awe as the flickering candle serves as usher to the ghostly intruder.

Style and structure

Style

Julius Caesar is one of the simplest of Shakespeare's texts to study, and is manly and lucid. It contains a large proportion of public orations and private discussions, both highly emotional and making frequent use of hyperbole. As it is concerned with one man who was a world figure and another who was the soul of honour, exaggeration is inevitable. Belonging to the 'middle period' it has fewer figurative expressions than the greater tragedies; it relies more on key words, repeated deliberately for emphasis or less consciously, out of angry passion.

Key words

Most conspicuous, as might be expected, is 'blood' and its associated forms, found mostly in Acts II and III. Blood from celestial combat was seen to drizzle down on the Capitol, while Calphurnia (according to her husband) saw a statue of him spouting blood from a hundred orifices – interpreted by Decius as life-giving streams with which to revive Rome. Caesar boasts of having no ordinary blood, certainly not the rebel blood that yields too easily. When he has been slain his blood reddens the hands and fingers of the murderers and is then smeared on their weapons; Antony grieves over it as 'most noble', 'sacred' and 'costly' (III, 1); to the commoners the much-stabbed corpse is a 'bloody sight', over which Antony evokes the public spectacle of Pompey's statue running with blood, and the more intimate image of the personified blood opening a door to see who was knocking.

In Act V, on the other hand, where there is much bloodshed off-stage and three corpses on-stage, the only references are the (second) mention of the blood from a horse's flanks when urged on by the spur and, a rare poetic touch, the red blood of Cassius, the instigator of all this, reflected (as seen by his devoted follower) in the red rays of the setting sun. Inevitable, perhaps, is the comparison with *Macbeth*: to Macbeth and his lady spilt blood is evidence of their great crime, to be scrubbed and scrubbed from their hands; in *Julius Caesar* it is a sacred symbol spread over the conspirators' forearms as a mark of their devotion to freedom.

'Honour' has been dealt with under *Theme*. 'Constancy' is another prized quality of character, whether firm determination in Caesar, endurance of pain by Portia, the outward calm assumed by the 'faction' in daylight, or the refusal to panic impressed by Brutus on Cassius. Its opposite, 'fear', comes in all its forms, from a state of 'servile fearfulness' under a tyrant to the ultimate fear of death (ended only by death itself); examples are Brutus's fear of an unwelcome event, such as the crowning of Caesar, Cassius's fear of Antony, Calphurnia's fear of omens, Caesar's suppressed fear of Cassius, the Senate's scramble to safety, the panicky crowds in the streets.

While hatred and suspicion are rife without any explicit reference to them, their opposite, 'love', is employed frequently for close and trustworthy friendship, and not (with the exception of Brutus and Portia) that special relationship between the sexes for which it is predominantly used today. That comradeship is put to the test when Antony finds it expedient to shake the hands of the assassins and when Titinius finds Cassius dead through a misunderstanding of what had happened to him. The greatest and most enduring affection is that between Brutus and Cassius; the depth and dramatic passion of their quarrel are testimony to it. That incident showed that what attracted others to Brutus was not so much his honesty as his gentleness in an age of violence and treachery. His reputation as a man of honour was simply a banner to fight under.

Verse

Rhythm (measured movement) in verse or prose is created when a certain arrangement of stressed and unstressed syllables satisfies the ear. It helps a poet to create emotion.

Metre defines the rhythm of each line of verse by the number and nature of its 'feet': (1) *iambic*, two syllables with the stress on the second (×/); (2) *trochaic*, two syllables with the stress on the first (/×); (3) *anapaestic*, three syllables with the stress on the last (××/); (4) *dactylic*, three syllables with the stress on the first. The bulk of English verse and of Shakespeare's plays is in 'verses' of five iambic feet, called iambic pentameters; where these are unrhymed, they constitute 'blank verse'.

Rhyme

This is strictly 'rime', misspelt through confusion with 'rhythm'. It is the agreement (sometimes approximate) in sound of the final syllables of two or more lines; the rhyming vowels should be preceded by different consonants. Much of Shakespeare's early work is in rhymed couplets; in *Julius Caesar* they are used only to mark the close of a scene or an important exit, as in I,2,318–9, 'sure . . . endure'; II,3,13–4, 'live . . . contrive' (imperfect); V,3,89–90, 'part . . . heart'; V, 5, 50–1, 'still . . . will'; V,5, 80–1, 'away . . . day'. The only other rhyme is that of the 'cynic' (IV,3,130–1)!

Prose

In Shakespeare's plays, except for the comedies, prose is usually a departure from verse, sometimes filling out whole scenes, at others reflecting changes of mood or differences in character. It is particularly used by comic characters, of whom we have one in the Cobbler, whose wisecracks alternate with the verse rebukes of the Tribunes. Less prominent, but a definite character, is the Fourth Plebian in Act III Scene 2, yet he and his fellows utter a mixture of verse and prose.

As a rule Shakespeare's prose-speakers, again outside the comedies, are people of lower social position than the nobility; theirs is assumed to be of an inferior plane of feeling to that of the leading characters. In *Julius Caesar* the small proportion of prose has two special purposes: (1) Casca's cynical flippancy in Act I Scene 2 comes across best in the broken cadences of prose; (2) Brutus's studied oratory, with its antitheses, elaborate climaxes and rhetorical questions, is stiff enough without added regularity of stress. One wonders when and where this meticulously prepared thesis was put together! His short iambic line, as he ascends the rostrum, allows for a pause, as if he were stopping to take out his notes, 'Be patient till the last' (no interruptions, please!). As soon as he has descended he reverts to his normal verse, 'Good countrymen, let me depart alone.'

Structure

The five Acts of Elizabethan drama are, appropriately in the case of *Julius Caesar*, of Roman origin, the chief influence being some poetic tragedies by Seneca the Younger (4 BC – AD 65), almost all that survived of Latin tragedy. Shakespeare would have read an English translation of 1581. Besides the division into five *actus*, *primus* to *quintus* as in the Shakespeare Folio, they contained long rhetorical speeches and the appearance of ghosts. Much Roman literature was modelled on Greek works, and the five acts correspond to the development of an Athenian play through a prologue, three episodes and an exodus, which division has formed the basis of a theory of dramatic construction:

1 Exposition, or introduction of the main characters.
2 Entanglement, or involvement of the characters in the (main) plot.
3 Crisis, or highest point of tension in the minds of the audience.
4 Denouement, or disentanglement from the complication.
5 Resolution, or winding-up of the action.

In addition Greek productions observed as far as possible three 'dramatic unities': time (24 hours), place (one scene), and action (one main plot i.e. no sub-plot and no blending of tragedy and comedy). These were the rules of classical drama, more closely followed on the Continent than in England. Elizabethan stage performances had taken shape as a succession of short scenes at various times and in different places, having grown partly out of the early miracle plays (today being resurrected) with their procession of vehicles and fifteen minute shows.

The third 'unity', of action, has largely been realized, as there is no subplot and only shreds of comic relief. In spite of a remarkable variety of rhetorical outbursts that often impede action, while revealing character or concealing the passage of time, in spite indeed of a large *dramatis personae*, the conduct of events is an outstanding example of Shakespeare's dramatic genius. He departed, like his contemporaries, from the classical custom of keeping death off the stage, such happenings being reported by a 'messenger'. Yet Antony's (imaginary) account of the assassination, as he holds up the much-rent robe, has perhaps more impact than the recent scrimmage with flourished swords and the splashing of blood.

A 'tragedy' has not only its special construction, it has also a special meaning, dissociated from daily disasters in the newspaper world. It has been variously defined – simplest is the idea of sheer waste of fine qualities by one overriding weakness or fatal obsession, not the actual death of a 'hero' (chief character). Caesar's greatness was wasted by a planned murder, based largely on jealousy; Brutus's honourable career was cut short by participation in a crime. Shakespeare's habit of balancing good and evil is seen also in the gaining of 'freedom' being marred by consequent sordid haggling and bitter quarrelling. His own attitude, discreetly 'veiled', towards problems of human life and conduct may perhaps be glimpsed in the occasional shafts of irony, especially dramatic irony, as when, surrounded by the crouching pack, Caesar pontificates:

> I do know but one
> That *unassailable* holds on his rank,
> Unshak'd of motion: and that I am he
> Let me a little show it. (III, 1,68–71)

The soliloquy

Such fixity of mind on Caesar's part calls for little thinking aloud, in the form of the soliloquy, which was a favourite recourse by Elizabethan dramatists, but supremely by Shakespeare, for revealing to an audience motives, hopes and fears, desires and dislikes that could not be conveyed by action or dialogue, or not sufficiently so; it is rare in modern productions. During the year before the appearance of *Julius Caesar*, the most famous soliloquy of all, 'thou idol ceremony', had been put into the mouth of Henry V, in the middle of a battlefield at dead of night. Its success led to a good many more. In Act II, Scene 1 Brutus communes (intermittently) with himself (and the audience) on swelling ambition, the state of Rome, and the conspiratorial look. In the same scene we hear an echo of King Henry's envy of the peasant's undisturbed slumbers when Brutus muses over the recumbent Lucius:

Enjoy the honey-heavy dew of slumber;
Thou hast no figures nor no fantasies
Which busy care draws in the brains of men. (II, 1,230–2)

(At Sardis the 'honey-heavy dew' has become a 'leaden mace').

Soliloquies by two other main characters have instantaneous effects upon the sympathies of their audience: Cassius admits having seduced Brutus from an honourable loyalty to his benefactor, but he is honest about it, comparing himself unfavourably:

> therefore 'tis meet
> That noble minds keep ever with their likes. (I, 2,307–8)

Antony's few words, after a long harangue eliciting tears for the dead, are more shocking: having transformed an anxious crowd of plebians into a howling mob, he merely makes the sinister comment:

> Mischief, thou art afoot,
> Take thou what course thou wilt. (III, 2,262–3)

He has perverted the crowd against Brutus as Cassius perverted Brutus against Caesar. What he means by 'mischief' he has already portrayed in the prophecy over Caesar's dead body. This forecast should prepare the audience for the reality of Antony's strategy. Cassius acted out of envy. Antony is motivated by revenge. He asks forgiveness of the dead body and then envisages a destructive and pitiless civil war with Caesar's *spirit* leading a hunt against his murderers.

General questions plus questions on related topics for coursework/examinations on other books you may be studying

1 Write an essay on Shakespeare's use of animal life and natural phenomena in *Julius Caesar*.

Suggested notes for essay answer:

Warwickshire boyhood made Shakespeare a nature lover though not an expert on wildlife – more interest in appearance, movements, character and value as symbols – most of his plays have references throughout to animals, birds and reptiles – some attractive, some sinister.

Rome and Asiatic provinces unfamiliar countryside – relied on reading in Plutarch and elsewhere – in England lion in a cage or on royal arms, whereas Rome had numbers that fought in the arena (Caesar and 'danger') – single lion and lioness used as symptoms of storm.

Animal characteristics – fawning of spaniel – cowardice of cur – motiveless barking at the moon – gentleness of lamb – buzzing of angry bees – brave fight of stag against pack – hunting of bears, elephants and legendary unicorn.

Omens in sacrificed birds (misunderstood as 'beast' in II,2,40) – omens in activities of wild birds – good in eagles, bad in scavengers.

Analogies from: adder – danger of its 'sting' avoided by crushing the egg – ass used as burden bearer – horses that begin by prancing but collapse when charging.

Omens in weather: comets and princes' deaths – storms and anger of gods – capricious striking of lightning; **Stars** – one constant in North Star – fortunes not determined by stars – analogy of ship sailing with the tide to make a fortune.

2 Describe Caesar as seen by (a) Decius Brutus, (b) Marcus Brutus, (c) Antony.

3 Do you think that Shakespeare regarded the assassination as a crime, fittingly punished?

4 Give in your own words the substance of the two funeral speeches.

5 How far does the 'spirit' of Caesar influence the course of the drama?

6 Illustrate from the play (a) the atmosphere of ancient Rome as created by the dramatist, and (b) the limitations imposed by the period in which he lived.

7 What references are made to events and incidents involving Caesar before the opening of the play, and with what purposes are they introduced?

8 Comment on the use of stage humour in this play, and distinguish three different kinds, criticizing their suitability for the occasion.

9 Which of the two conspirators, Brutus and Cassius, appeals to you more? Give your reasons.

10 What qualities in Brutus unfitted him for (a) conspiracy, (b) leadership?

11 How many different acts of revenge can you find in this play?

12 Which two speeches (a) exercised most influence on the action, and which two (b) revealed most intimately the real characters of the speakers?

13 How did individual conspirators, apart from the two leaders, contribute to the success of the undertaking?

14 Describe in some detail what you consider the best example of (a) loyalty, (b) treachery.

15 Why do you think Shakespeare gave the citizens a much greater part in the play than the Senate?

16 What would be lost if the women's parts were omitted?

17 Tell the story as Lucius would see it.

18 What changes came over Cassius towards the end?

19 You are dull, Casca, and those sparks of life
That should be in a Roman you do want,
Or else you use not.

Explain this utterance from the immediate circumstances, and compare it with what you know of Casca.

20 What use is made in *Julius Caesar* of (a) dreams, (b) omens, (c) philosophy?

21 Would you agree that destiny seems more overwhelming in this than in any other Shakespeare play?

22 How would you set the stage and group the actors for Act III, Scene 1 and 2?

23 'A mob is a collective bully made up of individual cowards.' Does this modern definition fit the crowd in *Julius Caesar*? Give your reasons.

24 'Et tu, Brute?' Why do you think this was expressed in

Latin? Mention other equally terse and significant phrases, relating them to their contexts.

25 What features make this play especially suitable for film production?

26 'The most splendidly written political melodrama we possess.' (G. B. Shaw, by no means biased towards Shakespeare). What lessons has *Julius Caesar* for the twentieth century?

27 Describe a struggle for power or a rebellion in any book you are studying.

28 Describe in some detail the most dramatic incident in a play or story you have read recently.

29 Write about a speaker in a story or play you know well who influences his/her audience in a particular way.

30 Show how an author uses the theme of corruption in one or more books.

31 Describe a character in your chosen book who yields to temptation.

32 Examine the imagery in a book you know well and say what it contributes to our appreciation.

33 Indicate the parts played by any two or three minor characters in a play or novel you are studying.

34 Describe a humorous incident in an otherwise sad or tragic story.

35 Compare any important character in *Julius Caesar* with the leading character in one of your books.

Further reading

Books on Shakespeare, and especially on *Julius Caesar*, are legion. First Folios, some in reduced facsimile, should be available in central reference libraries.

Editions: by J. Dover Wilson in the New Cambridge Edition, 1949
by T. S. Dorsch in the New Arden Edition, Methuen, 1955
by N. Sanders in the New Penguin Edition, 1967

Criticism:
Sir Walter Raleigh, *Shakespeare, English Man of Letters*
A. C. Bradley, *Shakespearian Tragedy* (Macmillan, 1904, 1957)
F. E. Halliday, *Shakespeare* (Thames & Hudson, 1964)
Derek Traversi, *Shakespeare: Roman Plays* (Hollis & Carter, 1963)

Reference: E. K. Chambers, *William Shakespeare* (OUP, 1930)
ed. O. J. Campbell & E. G. Quinn, *A Shakespeare Encyclopaedia*
   (Methuen, 1966)
G. & B. Lloyd Evans, *Everyman's Companion to Shakespeare* (Dent, 1978, 1981)